THE
COMMONSENSE
COOKERY BOOK

BOOK ONE REVISED EDITION

THE COMMONSENSE COOKERY BOOK

BOOK ONE REVISED EDITION

Revised by the trustees of the NSW
Cookery Teachers' Scholarship Fund

Angus&Robertson
An imprint of HarperCollins*Publishers*

Angus&Robertson
An imprint of HarperCollins*Publishers*, Australia

This paperback edition first published in Australia by
Angus & Robertson Publishers in 1970
Reprinted in 1971, 1972, 1973
Metric edition 1974
Reprinted 1975, 1976, 1977, 1978 (twice), 1979, 1981, 1982(twice),
1983, 1984 (twice), 1985, 1987
Revised edition 1988
Reprinted in 1989, 1990, 1991 (twice), 1992, 1994 1995

HarperCollins*Publishers*
25 Ryde Road, Pymble, Sydney, NSW 2073, Australia
31 View Road, Glenfield, Auckland 10, New Zealand

National Library of Australia Cataloguing-in-Publication data:

The commonsense cookery book, Book 1..
   New ed.
   Includes Index.
   ISBN 0 207 15656 5.
   1. Cookery.
   I. New South Wales Public School Cookery Teachers' Association.
641.5

Internal illustration by Linda Arnold and Liz Seymour
Typeset in 10/11pt Garamond by Midland Typesetters, Maryborough
Printed in Australia by The Book Printer, Victoria

30 29 28 27
98 97 96 95

FOREWORD

The development of the Australian Dietary Guidelines by the Commonwealth Department of Health was a response to a need to promote good health practices, and help prevent obesity and diseases such as heart diseases that are common among Australian adults.

In this edition of the *Commonsense Cookery Book*, recipes have been added, and current recipes, which have been revised to support the Guidelines, provide for flexibility in the use of recipes by:

- Using butter, margarine and oils of all varieties as substitutes for one another.

- Using non-fat skim milks and yoghurts instead of the full-cream varieties.

- Reducing the amount of, or deleting sugar and salt as desired.

- Making use of a variety of herbs and/or condiments to increase the palatability of dishes in which salt had previously been used.

- Choosing from the increased number of dishes in the savoury section, which have as their major ingredient, foods from the "eat most", section of the Healthy Diet Pyramid.

- Choosing from the greater number of fish, chicken and salad recipes.

CONTENTS

BASIC KITCHEN REQUISITES

A reliable stove
Saucepans of various sizes
Double saucepan
Boiler and steamer
Pressure cooker
Baking dish and trivet
Frying pan
Frying basket
Omelette pan
Griller or gridiron
Ovenproof dishes
Pie dish
Microwave dishes
Dishwasherproof dishes
Moulds
Pudding basins
Mixing bowls
Cake tins
Sandwich tins (pair)
Swiss roll tin
Set of scales
(*imperial and metric*)
Set of standard measures
Set of skewers

Set of cutters
(*pastry and biscuit*)
Strainers
Sifter
Chopping board
Pastry board or sheet
Rolling pin
Pastry brush
Grater
Egg whisk
Fish slice
Potato masher
Flour scoop
Flour dredge
Wooden spoon
Basting spoon
Kitchen fork
Corkscrew
Tin-opener
Pair of scissors
Oven holder
Clock
Storage jars
Cake cooler

THE HEALTHY DIET
PYRAMID

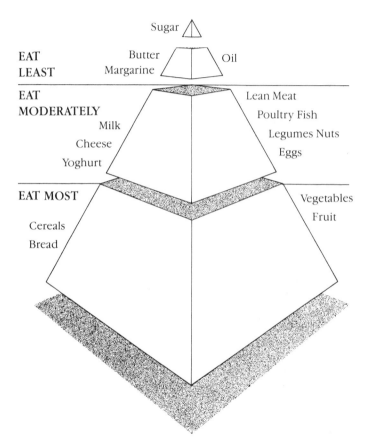

Sugar

**EAT
LEAST**
Butter
Margarine
Oil

**EAT
MODERATELY**
Milk
Cheese
Yoghurt
Lean Meat
Poultry Fish
Legumes Nuts
Eggs

EAT MOST
Cereals
Bread
Vegetables
Fruit

*The Healthy Diet Pyramid (reproduced with permission of the Australian Nutrition
Foundation) shows how much of each food type should be selected and is a
recommended guide for planning meals and shopping.*

STANDARD FRACTIONAL
MEASURING CUPS

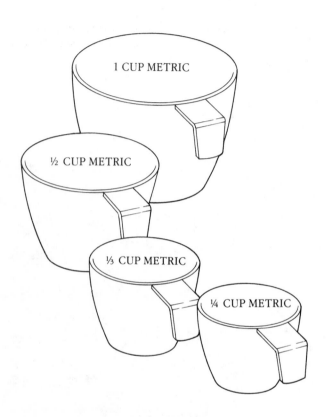

ACCEPTED LIQUID CONVERSIONS

1 gill	150 ml	¾ cup
½ pint	300 ml	1¼ cups
1 pint	600 ml	2½ cups
1 quart	1 l + 200 ml	5 cups
1 gallon	4 l + 800 ml	20 cups

METRIC CUP & SPOON
MEASUREMENTS

All measurements in this book conform to the metric cup and
spoon measurements of the Standards Association of Australia.

1 metric cup	250 ml
1 tablespoon	20 ml
1 teaspoon	5 ml

Spoon measures are *level* spoonfuls.

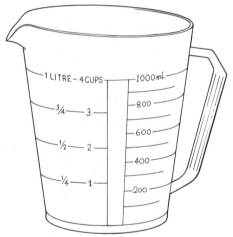

½ TEASPOON 2.5ml

TEASPOON 5ml

1.25ml ¼ TEASPOON

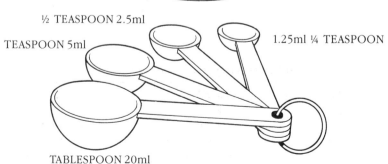

TABLESPOON 20ml

METRIC CONVERSIONS
LENGTH MEASUREMENTS

mm	cm	inches
2		1/16
3		⅛
5		¼
10	1	½
20	2	¾
25	2.5	1
50	5	2
62	6	2½
	8	3
	10	4
	15	6
	18	7
	20	8
	23	9
	25	10
	30	12
	35	14
	40	16
	45	18
	50	20

TEMPERATURES

100 degrees Celsius (boiling point) = 212 degrees Fahrenheit
0 degrees Celsius (freezing point) = 32 degrees Fahrenheit

CELSIUS (C.) INTO FAHRENHEIT (F.)

deg. C.	deg. F.	deg. C.	deg. F.
120	248	200	392
130	266	210	410
140	284	220	428
150	302	230	446
160	320	240	464
170	338	250	482
180	356	260	500
190	374		

For oven temperatures degrees Celsius approximately
equal half of degrees Fahrenheit.

	WARM		MODERATE		HOT		VERY HOT	
°C	150	160	180	190	200	220	230	250	260
°F	300	325	350	375	400	425	450	475	500

ROASTING AND BAKING
WITH A MEAT THERMOMETER

MEAT		TEMPERATURE °C
Beef	rare	60
	medium	70
	well done	75
Lamb	medium	75
	well done	80
Mutton	well done	80
Veal	well done	75
Fresh pork	well done	85
Cured pork	well done	75
Tender Ham	well done	65
Whole poultry	well done	85
Boneless poultry	well done	75

Note: *These temperatures only act as a guide; it is often stated that they are too low for Australian tastes.*

The shaft of the thermometer should be placed in the thickest part of the meat, not touching the bone.

BEEF

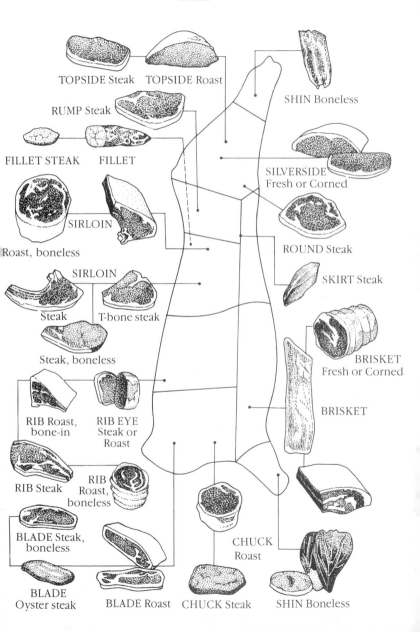

TOPSIDE Steak TOPSIDE Roast

SHIN Boneless

RUMP Steak

FILLET STEAK FILLET

SILVERSIDE
Fresh or Corned

SIRLOIN

ROUND Steak

Roast, boneless

SKIRT Steak

SIRLOIN

Steak T-bone steak

Steak, boneless

BRISKET
Fresh or Corned

BRISKET

RIB Roast,
bone-in

RIB EYE
Steak or
Roast

RIB Steak RIB
Roast,
boneless

BLADE Steak,
boneless

CHUCK
Roast

BLADE
Oyster steak

BLADE Roast CHUCK Steak SHIN Boneless

LAMB

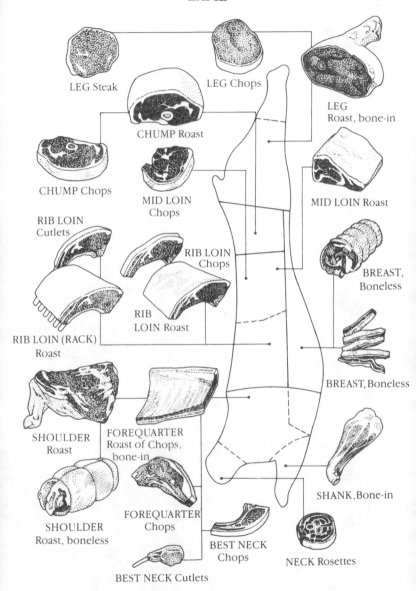

LEG Steak

LEG Chops

LEG Roast, bone-in

CHUMP Roast

CHUMP Chops

MID LOIN Chops

MID LOIN Roast

RIB LOIN Cutlets

RIB LOIN Chops

BREAST, Boneless

RIB LOIN Roast

RIB LOIN (RACK) Roast

BREAST, Boneless

SHOULDER Roast

FOREQUARTER Roast of Chops, bone-in

SHANK, Bone-in

SHOULDER Roast, boneless

FOREQUARTER Chops

BEST NECK Chops

NECK Rosettes

BEST NECK Cutlets

PORK

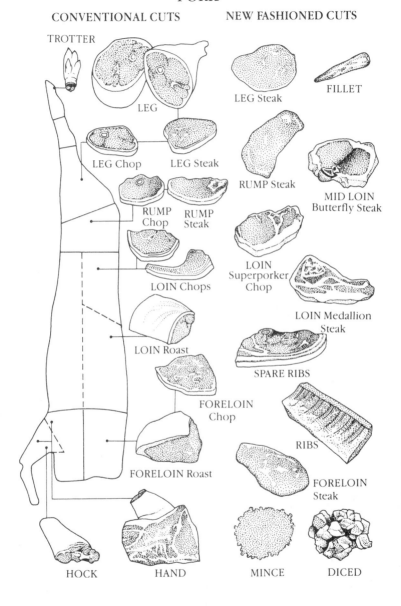

CONVENTIONAL CUTS

TROTTER

LEG

LEG Chop   LEG Steak

RUMP Chop   RUMP Steak

LOIN Chops

LOIN Roast

FORELOIN Chop

FORELOIN Roast

HOCK   HAND

NEW FASHIONED CUTS

LEG Steak   FILLET

RUMP Steak   MID LOIN Butterfly Steak

LOIN Superporker Chop   LOIN Medallion Steak

SPARE RIBS

RIBS

FORELOIN Steak

MINCE   DICED

LAMB

COOKERY METHOD	MEAT CUTS	TIME
BOIL AND SIMMER	Leg—plain.	Place in boiling water. Reduce heat to simmer steadily for 60 minutes per kg.
	Leg—pumped or cured.	Place in cold water, bring to boil and reduce to simmer until tender.
SOUP	Shanks. Scrag neck.	2 hours minimum.
Note: Hogget and Mutton	Same as lamb.	Increase cooking time ⅓ – ½.
TONGUE		2–3 hours or until tender.

TEMPERATURE	TRADITIONAL ACCOMPANIMENTS
	Boiled root vegetables. Parsley, onion or caper sauce.
Medium to Low– Medium. Gentle simmer.	Chopped parsley.
Same as for lamb.	Same as for lamb.
Medium to Low– Medium. Gentle simmer.	Served hot: boiled root vegetables. Parsley, mustard or onion sauce.

LAMB

COOKERY METHOD	MEAT CUTS	TIME
ROAST Large or thick cuts	Leg. Chump leg. Loin. Crown roast. Rack.Forequarter.Forequarter boned and rolled. Shoulder. Shoulder boned and rolled. Rolled breast.	60 minutes per kg. If meat is seasoned and rolled allow an extra 30 minutes cooking time.
GRILL, FRY OR BARBEQUE Chops, cutlets and steaks	Leg steak or chops. Lamb chump chops. Loin chops. Rib cutlets and chops. Forequarter chops. Shoulder chops.	Vertical or flat grill: 12–16 minutes. Fried cutlets: 8–12 minutes. Plain, crumbed or barbecue: 8–15 minutes (depends on distance from glowing coals).
CASSEROLE BRAISE AND STEW	Chump chops. Best neck, round neck chops. Shoulder chops. Shanks.	1½–2 hours gentle simmer.

TEMPERATURE	TRADITIONAL ACCOMPANIMENTS
160–180°C *Thermometer:* 83°C	**LAMB** Mint sauce. Thin brown gravy. Baked vegetables. **MUTTON** Red currant jelly. Thin brown gravy. Baked vegetables.
High–Medium down to Medium. Turn often and adjust position in relation to heat.	Steamed vegetables. Salad. Tomato halves. Potato chips. **CUTLETS** Bacon rolls. Green butter. Tomato halves. Potato chips.
Medium to Low–Medium.	Mashed or jacket potato. Casseroled, boiled, steamed or microwaved carrots and green vegetables. Chopped parsley.

BEEF

COOKERY METHOD	MEAT CUTS	TIME
ROAST Large or thick cuts	Yearling silverside and topside. Rolled sirloin. Sirloin roast. Rolled rib. Standing rib. Bolar blade.	60 minutes per kg. 40 minutes per kg for medium-rare.
GRILL, FRY OR BARBEQUE Steak	Yearling silverside. Topside and round. Rump. Fillet. Sirloin. T-Bone. Porterhouse. Scotch fillet. Rib. Oyster blade. Yearling blade.	Grill: 7–15 minutes. Fry: 10–20 minutes. Hotplate: 7–15 minutes. Over glowing coals: 7–20 minutes. Vertical grill: 7–15 minutes.
BRAISE, STEW OR CASSEROLE Steak	Topside. Round. Skirt. Chuck. Gravy beef (minced).	4 servings, minimum of 2 hours.
SIMMER Large cuts	Corned silverside. Rolled rib corned. Rolled brisket corned. H bone corned.	80 minutes per kg
SOUPS Brawn	Ox tail. Gravy beef. Shin (bone in).	Minimum 2 hours

TEMPERATURE	TRADITIONAL ACCOMPANIMENTS
160–180°C *Thermometer:* Well done 77°C; rare to medium 65–70°C.	Yorkshire pudding. Horseradish sauce. Thin brown gravy. Baked vegetables.
High–Medium down to Medium. Adjust distance from heat OR position on heated base.	*Grill and fry* Parsley butter. Potato chips. Grilled tomato. Tossed salad. *Barbecue* Jacket potatoes. Sliced onions, mushrooms. Tossed salad.
Medium to Low.	Chopped parsley.
Medium steady simmer.	Boiled root vegetables. Suet dumplings. Parsley, mustard or onion sauce.
Medium steady simmer.	Chopped parsley. Croutons.

PORK

COOKERY METHOD	MEAT CUTS	TIME
ROAST Large thick cuts	Leg. Loin. Boned rolled loin Shoulder. Foreloin or cushion. Spring or belly (rolled). Shoulder.	100 minutes per kg 80 minutes per kg 80 minutes per kg 90 minutes per kg
GRILL, FRY OR BARBEQUE *Remove rind before cooking.*	Chump chops. Leg steaks. Forequarter chops. Foreloin steak. Loin chops. Butterfly steak.	15–20 minutes 10–15 minutes 15–20 minutes 10–15 minutes 15–20 minutes 5–20 minutes
STEW OR BRAISE	Leg steak. Chump chops. Spare ribs—plain or marinated. Diced belly. Foreloin chops.	3–5 minutes to brown meat and 20–40 minutes in sauce or gravy.
BOIL AND SIMMER	Cured leg or ham. Pickled hand. Cured and smoked cushion (bacon).	60 minutes per kg

TEMPERATURE	TRADITIONAL ACCOMPANIMENTS
160–180°C *Thermometer*: Boneless pork 76°C; with bone 85°C.	Apple sauce. Thick brown gravy. Sage and onion seasoning. Baked vegetables.
Moderate heat—turn often. Adjust distance from heat or position on heated base.	Apple. Pineapple rings. Potato chips. Boiled, steamed, microwaved root and green vegetables. Tossed salad.
Moderate heat	Chopped parsley. Selection of vegetables suitably cooked. Boiled or savoury rice or boiled pasta.
Place in cold water to cover; bring to boil then reduce heat and simmer.	Boiled root vegetables. Mustard, apple or horseradish sauce.

VEAL

COOKERY METHOD	MEAT CUTS	TIME
ROAST	Topside or leg silverside. Shoulder. Boned and rolled shoulder or forequarter.	80 minutes per kg, 90 minutes per kg if rolled and filled with seasoning.
FRY **GRILL** **BRAISE** **CASSEROLE**	Round, silverside or rump steaks Chops Cutlets	Shallow fry. 5–10 minutes. Grill 7–10 minutes. Fry 5–10 minutes. Casserole 1–1½ hours.
STEW	Knuckle neck	1½ hours
SOUP	Shank	1½ hours

TEMPERATURE	TRADITIONAL ACCOMPANIMENTS
160–180°C *Thermometer*: 77°C	Boiled ham or bacon. Thick brown gravy. Slices of lemon. Forcemeat or seasoning. Baked vegetables.
High–Medium down to Medium.	Jacket or mashed potato. Boiled, steamed, casseroled or microwaved root and green vegetables. Chopped parsley (braise and casserole).
Medium steady simmer.	Jacket or mashed potato or dumplings or boiled pasta. Boiled, steamed or microwaved root and green vegetables. Chopped parsley.
Medium down to Low	Chopped parsley.

POULTRY

COOKERY METHOD	WHOLE AND CUTS	TIME
ROAST Whole	Turkey	3–3½ hours 5–6 kg bird 4–4½ hours 6½–8 kg bird
	Goose	50 minutes per kg
	Duck	40 minutes per kg
	Quail	20–30 minutes per kg
	Chicken	60 minutes per kg
FRY OR GRILL	Chicken Maryland Breast fillet Thigh and fillet Leg	10–15 minutes pan Hotplate Glowing grill
BRAISE, STEW OR CASSEROLE	Any piece with or without bone. Turkey Duck Chicken	Serving 4. 1–1½ hours according to size of pieces and amount of bone.

TEMPERATURE	TRADITIONAL ACCOMPANIMENTS
160°C on a stand 180°C on stand or rack 160–180°C on stand or rack 160°C on stand in dish or 160°C in vertical rack *Thermometer*: 83°C	*Turkey:* Rich brown gravy. Forcemeat balls. Bacon rolls. Lemon slices. *Duckling and Goose:* Brown gravy. Apple, orange or cherry sauce. *Chicken:* Bread or onion sauce. Grilled bacon. Brown gravy. Baked vegetables.
Low–Medium Temperature	Potato chips Tomato halves Crumbed banana/pineapple Corn fritters
Moderate heat, gentle simmer	Chopped parsley Boiled or savoury rice or pasta

POULTRY

COOKERY METHOD	WHOLE AND CUTS	TIME
STEAM OR SIMMER	Whole fowls (older birds).	Age will determine cooking time. Minimum 1 ½ hours. Test for tenderness
SOUPS	Necks. Body Carcase. Giblets (any bird).	In cold water bring to boil. Reduce to Low.

Note: Rabbit can be prepared and cooked in a manner similar to chicken

TEMPERATURE	TRADITIONAL ACCOMPANIMENTS
Simmer or in a steamer over steadily boiling water.	Boiled root vegetables. Parsley, bread, onion or caper sauce.
Gentle simmer	Chopped parsley Croutons

TERMS USED
IN COOKERY

Au gratin   A term applied to dishes prepared with or without
sauce, topped with breadcrumbs or grated cheese or both,
dotted with butter and browned in the oven or under the
griller.

Blanch   Plunge into boiling water briefly and drain, or cover
with cold water and bring to the boil and drain.

Blend   Combine ingredients with a spoon, using a wide
circular motion, and mix to a smooth paste using a cold
liquid.

Boiling point   100°C. When bubbles reach the surface of a
liquid and break.

Bouquet garni   A bunch of herbs consisting of 3 sprigs of
parsley, 2 sprigs of thyme, 1 sprig of marjoram and a bay
leaf tied together with a piece of string and placed in a
simmering sauce or stew. If dried herbs are used they should
be wrapped in a piece of wet cheesecloth, then tied, for easy
removal at the end of cooking time.

Caramel   Sugar cooked over moderate heat and stirred
constantly until it turns into a dark brown syrup. Used as
a colouring for soups, stews, gravies and sauces.

Compote   Fresh or dried fruit or vegetables cooked in syrup
and served cold.

Condensed milk   Whole milk concentrated by evaporating part
of the water content. It is available both sweetened and
unsweetened; the unsweetened form is known as evaporated
milk.

Croûtons   Small squares of bread fried in butter and served
with soup.

Dice   Cut into very small cubes.

Entrée   A small dish served before the main course.

Fillet   An undercut of meat; cut of meat or fish without skin or bone.

Fondant   A type of French confection; foundation for sweets.

Fricassee   A white stew using milk with stock.

Garnish   Ornament or decorate food.

Gâteau   A round, square or oval rich buttery cake or dough, decorated and served as a dessert.

Glaze   Brush over with liquid such as egg, milk, sugar and water, or aspic, to improve the appearance.

Haricot   A brown stew.

Knead   Blend a dough by first flattening it on a floured board and then turning the outside edge farthest from you to the centre, pressing down several times with the heels of your hands, pushing the dough away from you. The dough should then be turned a quarter of the way round, and the process repeated until the dough becomes satiny and elastic—generally after 5 to 10 minutes of energetic kneading.

Mask   Cover or coat with a thick sauce, or with aspic.

Maitre d'hôtel butter   Chopped parsley, lemon juice, and salt and pepper blended with softened butter or margarine and served with meat or fish.

Marinade   A highly seasoned liquid made of oils, herbs and vinegar in which meat or fish is soaked for some time to impart flavour and, sometimes, to tenderize.

Panada   A thick sauce used to bind meat or fish for rissoles or croquettes.

Purée   A pulp made by forcing cooked fruits or vegetables or other solid food through a strainer, or mashing them with a wooden spoon.

Sauté   Shake over heat in a little very hot butter or fat.

Shortening   Any animal or vegetable fat—butter, margarine, lard or dripping.

Simmering   80° to 85°C. When small bubbles form slowly and collapse below the surface.

Sippets   Small triangular-shaped pieces of dry toast.

Stock   A liquid made by simmering together meat bones or fish trimmings with vegetables and seasonings in water.
Tepid   Two parts of cold liquid to one part of boiling.
Zest   Thin, oil-bearing, coloured layer of citrus peel.

MICROWAVE COOKERY

Although the Microwave as well as the Conventional Methods have been provided for some recipes, a person with knowledge of microwave cookery may use the microwave oven to reduce time and energy and minimise the number of utensils when following recipes where only the conventional method is provided.

Some Hints for Microwave Cookery

1. Do not operate an empty microwave oven as the magnetron may be damaged.
2. Use only approved plastic film, a glass or china plate or kitchen paper to cover food whilst cooking.
3. Metal objects and dishes, and china dishes with gold or silver decoration may damage the oven.
4. If a fire starts in the oven, press the STOP pad, leave the door closed, turn off the power at the switch and pull out the plug.
5. Since the microwave wattage varies from oven to oven, charts will need to be consulted and cooking and standing times may need to be adjusted.
6. Slightly undercook first, test, then cook a few seconds longer if needed.

7. If microwave energy is shared among several dishes, cooking takes more time and allowance has to be made.
8. Skins of fruits and vegetables need to be pierced with a fork to prevent bursting.
9. Foods cook from the outside towards the centre so stir casseroles once or twice during cooking.
10. To soften pure icing sugar or brown sugar which has become lumpy, heat on HIGH for about 15 to 20 seconds.
11. To freshen the oven, add a few drops of detergent or vanilla essence to a tumbler of water and heat for 1 to 2 minutes. Wipe oven clean with a damp cloth.

VEGETABLES

Recommendations for Cooking

Boiling—Place in a small quantity of boiling water with the lid on the saucepan to prevent loss of nutriment. The quantity of salt added to the cooking water varies according to taste, or may be deleted. Liquid drained from cooked vegetables may be saved and used for stews or gravies.

Steaming—Any vegetable that is boiled may be steamed. Prepare as for boiling and place in a steamer over boiling water. Do not use salt—this may be added after cooking, according to taste. Generally, steamed vegetables require a little longer cooking time than boiled vegetables.

Microwave—Cooked in the microwave, vegetables retain their colour and nutrients better than boiled vegetables as they are cooked quickly and very little or no water is used. Skins are left on whenever possible and note should be taken on directions for cutting vegetables and placing a variety of these in the same dish when cooking. Never add salt and use a tightly fitting lid or microwave safe cling-wrap to hold in the steam. Standing time allows heat to penetrate the centre of the vegetable without overcooking the outer edges.

Baking—Hard vegetables can be placed in heated fat around the meat in a baking dish or in a separate dish. Turn during cooking for even colour and crispness.

Dry baking—Wash and dry, pierce the skin or wrap in foil, then place on oven shelf.

Young vegetables may be cooked by the following method: place prepared vegetables in saucepan with a tablespoon of butter or margarine and barely enough boiling water to cover base of saucepan. Cook gently with lid on until tender. Shake saucepan occasionally.

Frozen and tinned vegetables: follow instructions given by the manufacturer.

Dried Vegetables: Beans—haricot, lima, red kidney, soya beans.
Peas—split and whole dried peas.
Lentils—red and green lentils.

General cooking method—Wash well, drain, cover with cold water and soak up to 12 hours. Boil in the same water until tender. A little salt may be used when boiling. Drain and use in a variety of dishes.

CHEESE

Cheese has high nutritive value providing the essential nutrients protein, calcium, fat and phosphorus.

Skim-milk cheese contains less fat. It can be eaten in its natural state as a spread, as a dip, mixed in hot foods, and as a topping or garnish on hot or cold foods.

Purchasing and Storage

Let your personal taste guide you. Buy small quantities often; do not store too long. Dessert or soft cheese should be used immediately. Hard or grating cheese, for example, parmesan and romano, keep well for several months in a suitable container. Careful storage is important. Keep in the refrigerator wrapped in foil or film or replaced in original wrapper. Covered jars or self-sealing plastic containers should be used to store strongly flavoured cheese as the aroma will permeate other foods especially milk, butter, cream and eggs. A damp cloth wrung out in vinegar may be used to cover cheese kept in a cool place if refrigerator is not available.

AUSTRALIAN-MADE CHEESES	CONTINENTAL EQUIVALENTS
BLUE VEIN	–English Stilton, French Roquefort, Italian Gorganzola
CAMEMBERT	–French Camemberts—a soft-centred loaf
CHEDDAR	–English Cheddar well matured and firm
COLBY	–English Colby—softer and more open texture than cheddar
COTTAGE	–Farm. Unripened cheese varying in fat content
CREAM	–Neufchâtel or Philadelphia—unripened cheese, very high fat content

EDAM	–Dutch Edam—spiced varieties are available
FETTA	–Fetta—made from cows' milk in Australia. Ewes' milk in Greece, stored and matured in brine
GOUDA	–Dutch Gouda—smooth, firm and mellow
GRUYERE	–Swiss cheese
MOZZARELLA	–Italian mozzarella—made in pear shapes and hung on string. Soft, smooth, easy to grate. Favourite for pizza
PECARINO	–Italian pecarino—made from a mixture of cows' and ewes' milk, sometimes has black peppercorns mixed into the curd
PARMESAN	–Italian Parmesan—has a very long maturing time, has hard texture, pale yellow colour and is excellent for grating
RICOTTA	–Italian ricotta—made from the solids extracted from the whey of other cheeses. It is fresh and soft in texture, is sold in containers or bulk, does not keep for long periods
SWISS	–Swiss cheese—has a characteristic nutty flavour. It has holes or eyes made by the expansion of gas in the curd

Cooking

Cheese is a rich protein food which can be made unattractive and unpalatable by careless cooking. Cheese should be cooked in order to first soften and then melt. Too much heat will cause dry surface hardness or curdling stringiness in the moist heat of sauces. Excessive heat causes a separation of the fats. Best results are gained by moderate heat and short cooking time. Try to avoid reheating cheese dishes. Add grated cheese to cooked foods and sauces.

BREAKFAST COOKERY

FRUIT JUICE

INGREDIENTS

1 piece ripe citrus fruit

METHOD

1. Cut fruit through the thickest part.
2. Squeeze to remove juice.
3. Remove seeds and serve in a small glass.

MILK COFFEE

INGREDIENTS

1 tablespoon ground coffee
½ cup cold water
½ cup milk

METHOD

1. Put the coffee and water into a small saucepan, put the lid on, and bring slowly to simmering point.
2. Allow to stand 1 minute with lid on.
3. Strain through a fine strainer into a jug.
4. Heat the milk.
5. To serve, pour equal quantities of coffee and milk into the cup.

VARIATION

Add 1 teaspoon instant coffee to heated milk, water or milk and water.

Serves 1

TEA

INGREDIENTS

Use good quality tea-leaves

METHOD

1. Have water freshly boiled.

2. Rinse teapot with boiling water.

3. Allow 2 teaspoons tea-leaves to every 2½ cups of water or more, according to taste.

4. Pour boiling water on leaves and allow to infuse before pouring.

Serves 1

COCOA

INGREDIENTS

1 cup milk or ½ cup milk and ½ cup water
1 teaspoon cocoa
1 teaspoon sugar (optional)

METHOD

1. Heat milk or milk-and-water mixture.

2. Pour a little heated milk onto cocoa and sugar, and blend.

3. Return all to saucepan, heat slowly and simmer 1 minute.

Serves 1

FRUIT

Serve raw or cooked fruit for breakfast.

1. Fresh—whole or pieces.
2. Fruit salad.
3. Grilled—½ grapefruit.
4. Stewed (see cookery method p. 139.)

FRIED BACON

METHOD—CONVENTIONAL

1. Remove the rind from the bacon rashers, and save it to flavour soups, etc.

2. Place the bacon in frying pan.

3. Cook very slowly until the fat is transparent.

4. Drain on paper towel.

5. Serve very hot.

METHOD—MICROWAVE

1. Prepare as in Method 1 above.

2. Place bacon on a piece of paper towel on a plate.

3. Cover food with piece of paper towel.

4. Microwave for 3 minutes on HIGH.

FRIED BACON AND TOMATO OR MUSHROOM

INGREDIENTS

1 rasher of bacon
1 tomato
1 prepared mushroom
Pinch salt
Pinch pepper

METHOD—CONVENTIONAL

1. Remove rind from bacon.

2. Place bacon and mushroom in a cold pan without fat and fry slowly until fat is clear.

3. Lift on to a hot dish.

4. Wash and dry tomato, cut into thick slices or in half.

5. Place into the hot fat remaining after frying the bacon, cook slowly, turn only once and avoid breaking the slices, and sprinkle with salt and pepper.

6. Serve on rasher of bacon. Garnish with sprigs of parsley.

METHOD—MICROWAVE

1. Prepare as in Method 1 above.

2. Place bacon, tomato and mushroom on a piece of paper towel on a plate.

3. Cover food with a piece of paper towel.

4. Microwave on HIGH for 3 minutes.

Note: Tomato, mushroom and bacon may also be grilled.

Serves 1

EGGS COOKED IN SHELLS

There are three methods of lightly cooking eggs in shells:

1. Place eggs in boiling water and simmer gently for 3 minutes.

2. Place eggs in cold water, bring to the simmering point, and simmer for 1 minute. (Use this method for eggs taken from the refrigerator.)

3. Have saucepan of boiling water ready, place the eggs in, lift off the heat, and allow to remain from 6 to 10 minutes with lid tightly on.

FRIED EGG AND BACON

INGREDIENTS

1 rasher of bacon
1 egg

METHOD—CONVENTIONAL

1. Remove rind from bacon; put bacon in pan and cook until crisp.

2. Lift out and place on a hot plate.

3. If not sufficient fat in pan add a little margarine and make just warm.

4. Break the egg into a saucer and slide carefully into the warm fat.

5. Cook slowly, spoon fat over the egg while cooking.

6. When set, lift out with an eggslice, drain well, and place on the bacon.

METHOD—MICROWAVE

1. Remove rind from bacon, put bacon in custard cup or ramekin dish and cook for 1 minute on HIGH.

2. Place bacon on a hot plate.

3. Break egg into ramekin or custard cup, make 2 tiny incisions in the yolk with a sharp-pointed knife.

4. Cover with kitchen paper, cook for 30 seconds on HIGH or until eggwhite is set.

5. Slide onto bacon to serve.

Serves 1

EGG AND TOMATO

INGREDIENTS

1   tomato
1   dessertspoon butter
Salt and pepper to taste
1   egg
1   slice dry toast

METHOD

1. Wash and cut tomato up roughly.

2. Melt butter, and fry tomato for 3 minutes.

3. Add salt and pepper and simmer until tomato is cooked.

4. Place raw egg in hollow in cooked tomato.

5. Simmer gently until egg is set.

6. Slide onto a heated plate. Serve with toast.

Serves 1

STEAMED EGG

INGREDIENTS

1 egg
Buttered toast
Salt and pepper to taste

METHOD

1. Break egg and place in greased container.

2. Stand container over a pan of gently boiling water.

3. Cook slowly until set— about 4 minutes.

4. Slide onto buttered toast.

5. Garnish with parsley.

Serves 1

SCRAMBLED EGG

INGREDIENTS

1 teaspoon butter
1 egg
⅛ teaspoon salt
Pinch pepper
2 tablespoons milk
¼ teaspoon chopped parsley
1 slice hot buttered toast

METHOD—CONVENTIONAL

1. Melt butter in saucepan.

2. Beat egg well, add salt, pepper and milk; add to melted butter.

3. Stir over a gentle heat until thick, do not allow to become hard.

4. Remove from stove; add parsley.

5. Pile on hot toast on a hot plate.

METHOD—MICROWAVE

1. Whisk egg, milk, salt and pepper lightly with fork in serving bowl.

2. Cook on MEDIUM for 30 seconds, stirring once and then cook for a further 30 seconds.

3. Allow to stand 30 seconds to complete cooking.

4. Place butter and parsley on top before serving.

Serves 1

POACHED EGG

INGREDIENTS

½ teaspoon salt
6 drops vinegar
1 egg
1 slice buttered toast

METHOD—CONVENTIONAL

1. Put about 2.5 cm of water in a small frying pan or saucepan and bring to the boil.

2. Reduce temperature and add the salt and vinegar.

3. Break the egg into a saucer.

4. Drop the egg carefully into the water.

5. Allow to simmer slowly from 3 to 5 minutes, until set.

6. Lift the egg out with a spoon or slice, and drain.

7. Place carefully on the toast, and serve at once.

8. Garnish with chopped parsley.

METHOD—MICROWAVE

1. Place cup of water in oven at same time (for one egg only).

2. Break egg into muffin pan or custard cup.

3. Prick yolk and white, cook for 1 minute on MEDIUM.

4. Allow to stand while making toast.

5. Run knife around the edge and slip egg onto toast.

Serves 1

EGGFLIP

INGREDIENTS

1 fresh egg
1 teaspoon sugar
Flavouring
⅔ cup warmed milk

METHOD

1. Separate white from yolk of egg.

2. Mix yolk and sugar thoroughly.

3. Beat white until quite stiff.

4. Add yolk and sugar, then flavouring and milk.

5. Mix well.

6. Pour into a tumbler and serve.

VARIATION
Place all ingredients and ½ sliced banana in electric blender and mix until ingredients are combined. In summer use half milk and 1 heaped tablespoon of ice-cream.

Serves 1

7

ROLLED OATS

INGREDIENTS

1 cup rolled oats
1 cup water
Pinch salt (optional)
1½ cups near-boiling water

METHOD—CONVENTIONAL

1. Blend oats, water and salt in a saucepan.

2. Add near-boiling water, stir vigorously.

3. Boil 5 minutes stirring often until oatmeal mixture is thick and creamy.

4. Serve with a little honey, brown sugar or dried fruits.

METHOD—MICROWAVE

1. Place ⅓ cup oats to ⅔ cup water in porridge bowl.

2. Cook on HIGH for 1 minute.

3. Stir and cook on HIGH for another 1 minute, serve.

Note: Liquid can be milk, water or a mixture of both. A teaspoon of brown sugar, wheat germ or honey may be added before or after cooking.

VARIATION

Gruel may be made by substituting milk for water. Blend oatmeal with a little milk, boil remainder of milk and pour onto oatmeal, stir well, stand 1 minute; strain and simmer for 10 minutes before serving as a beverage in a cup with a little sugar and grated nutmeg on top.

Serves 4

BOILED RICE

INGREDIENTS

4 cups boiling or hot water
Pinch salt
½ cup white rice (this equals 1½ cups cooked rice)

METHOD—CONVENTIONAL

1. Put water and salt on to boil.

2. Wash rice.

3. Add to boiling water.

4. Cook quickly without lid until tender, approximately 15 minutes.

5. Strain.

Note: Brown rice requires longer cooking time—25 to 30 minutes.

METHOD—MICROWAVE

1. Place 1 cup rice to 2 cups water and salt in casserole dish, stir.

2. Cover with glass lid or kitchen paper, cook on HIGH for 10 minutes.

3. Stand 5 minutes before stirring with fork.

Serves 2

METHOD

1. Combine all ingredients, store in an airtight container.

2. Serve with low-fat yoghurt or skim milk.

3. Fresh fruit may be added when serving.

MUESLI

INGREDIENTS

4 cups instant rolled oats
4 tablespoons wheat germ
4 tablespoons unprocessed bran
2 teaspoons sunflower seeds
1 tablespoon chopped dried apricots
1 tablespoon sultanas
1 tablespoon chopped dried apples
1 tablespoon walnuts

STOCKS AND SOUPS

STOCK FOR CLEAR SOUP

INGREDIENTS

2 kg bones (beef, lamb, poultry)
2 teaspoons salt
3 litres cold water
1 carrot
1 turnip
1 brown-skinned onion
2 outside sticks celery
bouquet garni
1 dozen peppercorns
1 dozen cloves
1 blade mace

METHOD

1. Trim and wash the bones, remove the fat and marrow, and gash meat well.

2. Put bones, salt, meat and water into the stockpot or saucepan.

3. Allow to soak ½ to 1 hour.

4. Prepare the vegetables and cut up roughly; leave brown skin on the onion.

5. Add vegetables, bouquet garni, peppercorns, cloves, and mace.

6. Simmer gently 4½ hours in saucepan.

7. Remove bones and strain.

8. Allow to cool and remove the fat.

Note: If using a pressure cooker, reduce liquid to 6 cups, follow Method 1–5, bring to full pressure on high heat, reduce heat and cook with pressure for 15 minutes, then follow Method 7–8.

ECONOMICAL STOCK

Water in which fresh meat or vegetables has been boiled may be used as a foundation for many soups.

BROTH

INGREDIENTS

500 g scrag end of mutton
beef bones or knuckle of veal
2 litres water
season to taste
2 tablespoons pearl barley
1 carrot
1 onion
1 small turnip
1 stick celery
2 tablespoons finely chopped
parsley

METHOD

1. Wash meat.

2. Cut the meat off the bones, and remove fat.

3. Cut the meat into small pieces.

4. Put meat and bones into a saucepan with water and salt and pepper.

5. Wash the barley well in cold water, and add to saucepan.

6. Bring slowly to simmering point to extract the juices and flavour from the meat.

7. Wash and prepare the vegetables, and cut into small dice, and add them to the broth.

8. Simmer slowly 2 or 3 hours with lid on saucepan.

9. Take out the bones.

10. Remove fat with a spoon and absorb the remainder with paper towel laid on the surface.

11. Add parsley.

12. Serve hot.

Note: If using a pressure cooker reduce liquid to 4 cups, follow Method 1–7, pressure cook 15 minutes, then follow Method 9–12.

Serves 6

JULIENNE SOUP

INGREDIENTS

1 carrot
1 turnip
1 stick celery
1 tablespoon arrowroot
salt (optional)
5 cups stock or clear soup

METHOD—CONVENTIONAL

1. Wash and prepare vegetables.

2. Cut into thin strips like matches.

3. Cook the vegetables until tender in a little of the boiling stock or water.

4. Drain and keep warm.

5. Heat the remaining stock.

6. Mix the arrowroot with a little cold water.

7. Stir into the stock and stir until boiling.

8. Allow to cook for 3 or 4 minutes.

9. Add cooked vegetables and salt if required, and serve.

Note: Stock cubes may be used for making stock.

METHOD—MICROWAVE

1. Follow Conventional Method 1–2 above.

2. Microwave vegetables in a little of the boiling stock or water for 1 minute on HIGH.

3. As Conventional Method 4–6.

4. Stir into the stock, microwave for 1 minute on HIGH, stir well. Microwave 1 minute longer.

5. As Conventional Method 9.

Serves 4

FISH STOCK

INGREDIENTS

1 kg fish or fish bones
12 peppercorns
3 sprigs parsley
Rind of 1 lemon
1 onion
1 blade mace
2 teaspoons salt
2½ litres water

METHOD

1. Put all ingredients into a saucepan.

2. Bring slowly to the boil.

3. Simmer slowly 1 hour with lid on saucepan.

4. Strain.

Note: If using a pressure cooker reduce liquid to 5 cups and pressure cook for 15 minutes.

PEA SOUP

INGREDIENTS

1 cup split peas
3 litres cold water
Some bacon bones or rind
1 teaspoon dried mint
12 peppercorns
9 cloves
1 blade mace
1 large carrot
1 large turnip
1 onion
½ head celery
1 tablespoon flour

METHOD

1. Soak peas overnight in some of the cold water.

2. Place them in a large saucepan with the bacon, mint, and remaining water and peppercorns, cloves and mace tied in a muslin bag.

3. Bring slowly to the boil.

4. Prepare the vegetables; grate them or slice thinly.

5. Add to saucepan and cook slowly 3 hours with lid on. Remove muslin bag.

6. Rub through a coarse strainer or use a blender.

7. Blend the flour with cold water.

8. Return all to saucepan and bring to the boil.

9. Serve hot with small croutons of toast.

Note: If using a pressure cooker, reduce liquid to 1½ litres and pressure cook for 5 minutes. Consistency may be varied to taste by adding extra water.

Serves 6

MINESTRONE

INGREDIENTS

*1 cup dried beans (navy or
haricot)*
2½ cups cold water
2 rashers of bacon
*1 small clove garlic, finely
chopped*
1 medium onion, chopped
1½ cups diced carrots
1 cup diced celery
1 cup diced green pepper
2 teaspoons salt
¼ teaspoon pepper
5 cups stock or water
1 cup tomato pulp
½ teaspoon mixed herbs
1 tablespoon chopped parsley
1 cup finely shredded cabbage
½ cup green peas
⅓ cup cooked macaroni

METHOD

1. Soak beans in cold water overnight.

2. Remove rind from bacon, cut bacon into strips and fry in a large saucepan. Remove from saucepan.

3. Add garlic, onion, carrots, celery and green pepper to saucepan. Fry in bacon fat, stirring well for about 5 minutes—do not brown.

4. Add beans and water in which they have been soaking, salt, pepper, stock, tomato pulp and herbs.

5. Simmer 2 hours with lid on saucepan.

6. Add remaining ingredients except bacon.

7. Simmer again 30 minutes.

8. Serve garnished with fried bacon.

Note: If using a pressure cooker reduce combined amount of liquid to 4 cups, follow Method 1–4, pressure cook for 15 minutes, add remaining ingredients except bacon, pressure cook for 6 minutes and serve garnished with fried bacon.

Serves 6

TOMATO CREAM SOUP

INGREDIENTS

12 tomatoes or
2 × 425 g tins tomatoes
1 white onion
2½ cups stock or water
1 teaspoon salt
Bunch of fresh herbs if
available
1 teaspoon sugar
1¼ cups thin melted butter
sauce (see p. 224)
⅔ cup cream (optional)
Pepper to taste

METHOD—CONVENTIONAL

1. Slice tomatoes and cut onion finely.

2. Put in saucepan with stock, salt, herbs and sugar.

3. Cover and cook until onion is tender.

4. Puree when cool using a sieve or blender.

5. Gradually add this tomato puree to melted butter sauce and stir over low heat until hot but do not boil.

6. Add cream if liked. Add pepper to flavour as desired.

7. Serve with croutons.

METHOD—MICROWAVE

1. Place sliced tomatoes, chopped onion, stock, salt, herbs and sugar in a glass or china heat-resistant bowl, covered with a piece of kitchen paper or a glass plate.

2. Cook on HIGH for 15 minutes or until onion is tender.

3. Puree when cool using a sieve or blender.

4. Gradually add tomato puree to melted butter sauce and cook on HIGH for 1 minute—do not boil.

5. Add cream if liked. Add pepper to flavour as desired.

6. Serve with sippets.

Serves 6

VEGETABLE CREAM SOUP

INGREDIENTS

4 medium potatoes
1 onion
2 sticks celery
1 carrot
1 parsnip
1 turnip
2 tablespoons butter
2 teaspoons sugar
2 teaspoons salt
5 cups water
2½ cups milk
2 tablespoons flour
Salt and pepper to taste

METHOD—CONVENTIONAL

1. Wash vegetables.

2. Peel and cut up roughly.

3. Melt butter in a heavy saucepan, add vegetables, stir and cook without browning.

4. Add sugar, salt and water.

5. Boil gently 1 hour or until tender.

6. Rub through a sieve or use a blender.

7. Blend flour with a little cold milk, return with remainder of milk and vegetable pulp to the saucepan.

8. Stir and boil for 1 minute.

9. Season.

10. Serve hot with small croutons and chopped parsley.

METHOD—MICROWAVE

Follow Conventional Method but—

1. Use a glass or china heat-resistant bowl.

2. Cook covered with kitchen paper or a glass plate on HIGH for 10 minutes or until vegetables are soft, stirring mixture occasionally.

3. Heat, covered, on HIGH for 10 minutes, stirring occasionally.

4. Allow to stand for 2 or 3 minutes before serving.

Note: If using a pressure cooker reduce liquid to 3 cups water, follow Conventional Method 1–4 using the pressure cooker; bring to full pressure on hight heat; reduce heat and cook with pressure for 5 minutes; follow Conventional Method 6–10.

Serves 6

PUMPKIN SOUP

INGREDIENTS

½ kg pumpkin
1 large onion, chopped
2 chicken stock cubes
2 cups water
½ potato
Salt and pepper to taste
Grated nutmeg to taste

METHOD—CONVENTIONAL

1. Peel and chop pumpkin and potato.

2. Place in saucepan with water, chicken cubes and onion and boil until tender.

3. Puree when cool using a sieve or blender.

4. Combine the puree, salt, pepper and nutmeg.

5. Heat gently, serve sprinkled with chopped parsley and a swirl of yoghurt or sour or whipped cream if liked.

METHOD—MICROWAVE

1. Place peeled and chopped pumpkin, onion, water, chicken stockcubes in a large glass or china heat-resistant bowl, cover with paper towel or a glass plate.

2. Microwave on FULL for 15 minutes.

3. Puree when cool using a sieve or blender.

4. Stir in salt, pepper and nutmeg.

5. Reheat on MEDIUM or ROAST for 3 minutes.

6. Serve sprinkled with parsley and a swirl of yoghurt or sour or whipped cream if liked.

Note: Before serving soup consistency may be adjusted to taste by adding water. Soup may be served chilled or hot.

Serves 4

MULLIGATAWNY SOUP

INGREDIENTS

1   apple
1   onion
2   tablespoons butter, oil
or clarified fat
1   tablespoon curry powder
1   tablespoon chutney
2   teaspoons sugar
¼   cup lemon juice
2   tablespoons flour
2   litres stock
1   cup cooked rice

METHOD

1. Wash, dry apple and peel onion and cut roughly.

2. Fry in butter, fat or oil.

3. Add curry powder, chutney, sugar and lemon juice and cook gently 10 minutes.

4. Blend flour with a little stock, add with remainder of stock.

5. Simmer gently 1 hour.

6. Puree when cool using a sieve or blender.

7. Return to saucepan and reheat.

8. Serve rice in the soup.

Note: If using a pressure cooker reduce liquid to 1 litre and follow Method 1–4, pressure cook for 5 minutes and then follow Method 6–8.

Serves 6

BEETROOT SOUP

INGREDIENTS

2   large beetroot
2   onions
2   potatoes
1   parsnip
1   carrot
¼   cabbage heart
2   peeled tomatoes
2   litres beef stock
2   bay leaves

METHOD

1. Wash and peel beetroot, onions, potatoes, parsnip and carrot. Wash and drain cabbage.

2. Dice hard vegetables, slice tomatoes, chop cabbage.

3. Place all in a large heavy saucepan and simmer 1 hour.

4. Season to taste.

5. Serve hot with spoonful of sour cream or natural yoghurt.

In summer time

1. Stir the soup well and strain through fine strainer.

2. Chill well. Serve with spoonful of whipped cream cheese.

Serves 6

FISH

TO FILLET A FISH

METHOD

1. Place cleaned and scaled fish on paper on a firm surface.

2. Make an incision (with a pair of scissors or sharp knife) around the neck, up the middle of the back, across the tail, and up the belly, keeping as close to the fins as possible.

3. Loosen the skin around the head and holding skin with a paper towel in one hand, draw it off, holding the fish firmly by the head and being careful not to tear the flesh. Do this on both sides.

4. Cut down the middle of the back with a sharp knife.

5. Cut the flesh cleanly from the backbone on both sides, keeping the knife as close to the bone as possible.

6. Remove the small bones along the sides of the fish.

7. Cut flesh into 3 or 4 pieces according to the size of fish.

PAN-FRIED FISH

INGREDIENTS

1 small whole fish, cutlets or fillets per person
1 tablespoon flour
Pinch pepper
½ teaspoon salt
1 beaten egg or a little milk
Breadcrumbs
Enough melted fat
or oil to cover bottom of pan

METHOD

1. Trim, scale, wash and dry fish.

2. Roll fish in the combined flour, pepper and salt.

3. Dip in beaten egg or milk, and roll in breadcrumbs, pressing them on firmly.

4. Heat fat or oil until a blue haze begins to rise.

5. Cook slowly for 10 to 15 minutes or until flesh is white and tender, turning as necessary.

6. Drain on a paper towel.

7. Serve on a hot dish.

8. Garnish with slices of lemon and small sprigs of parsley.

STEAMED FISH

INGREDIENTS

Select suitable whole fish or fillets, according to number of serves required.
Juice of 1 lemon
Salt and cayenne pepper

METHOD—CONVENTIONAL

1. Clean, scale, wash and dry the fish; remove fins and trim the tail.

2. Wash in water to which has been added salt and a teaspoon of lemon juice (or a little vinegar) and pat dry.

3. Season and sprinkle with lemon juice, wrap in greased foil.

4. Oven steam or cook over gently boiling water for 10 to 20 minutes until fish is tender when tested through the thickest section.

5. Remove from foil and serve on a hot plate.

6. Garnish with lemon and parsley or dill or basil.

METHOD—MICROWAVE

Follow above method but place fish unwrapped in a shallow plate, cover with microwave-safe plastic wrap and cook on MEDIUM for 4 to 6 minutes, then stand for 2 minutes.

Note: Fish may be served with white sauce or a mixture of fish juices with lemon juice and herbs.

BAKED FISH

INGREDIENTS

1 large fish
Lemon juice
1 cup breadcrumbs (fresh)
1 tablespoon chopped parsley
A little grated lemon rind and nutmeg
1 tablespoon butter
¼ teaspoon salt
Pinch pepper
Milk

METHOD

1. Clean, scale, wash and dry the fish.

2. Remove the eyes.

3. Cut off the fins, and trim the tail.

4. Rub over inside and out with lemon juice.

5. Mix the breadcrumbs with all the other ingredients except the milk and a little of the butter.

6. Fill the fish with a portion of this, and sew with cotton or fasten with a skewer.

7. Grease a baking dish or line with greased paper or aluminium foil.

8. Place the fish in the dish and brush with milk.

9. Cover with remainder of seasoning, adding more breadcrumbs if necessary.

10. Put a few small pieces of butter on top.

11. Cover with greased paper or foil.

12. Bake in a moderate oven, 180–200°C, for 20 to 30 minutes or until flesh is tender in the thickest part near the head.

13. Fish is cooked when flesh is white and flakes easily.

14. Place on a hot dish with seasoning.

15. Garnish with sections of lemon and small sprigs of parsley.

Number of servings depends on size of fish.

SCALLOPED FISH

INGREDIENTS

*250 g cooked fish, canned fish
or oysters
⅔ cup thick basic white sauce
(see p. 224)
Few drops lemon juice
and tobasco sauce or herbs
Dried breadcrumbs
Butter or margarine*

METHOD

1. Combine fish, sauce and
seasonings.

2. Grease and crumb
scallop dish.

3. Place in the prepared
mixture, sprinkle
breadcrumbs on top.

4. Dot lightly with butter
or margarine.

5. Brown lightly in the
oven or under a griller.

6. Garnish with lemon and
parsley or dill.

Serves 2

GRILLED FISH

INGREDIENTS

*1 small fish or fillets per
person
Butter
Salt
Pepper*

METHOD

1. Clean and scale the fish.

2. Remove head and fins,
split open.

3. Wash, dry and brush
with oil or melted butter.

4. Grill lightly on both
sides.

5. Cook from 5 to 8
minutes according to
thickness. Fish is cooked
when flesh is white and
flakes easily.

6. Serve at once on a hot
plate.

7. Flavour with butter, salt
and pepper.

8. Garnish with lemon juice
and finely chopped parsley.

FISH MOULD

INGREDIENTS

1   cup cooked fish
1   egg
⅔ cup thick masking sauce
(see p. 224)
1 teaspoon chopped capers
Few drops lemon juice
1 tablespoon fresh
breadcrumbs

METHOD—CONVENTIONAL

1. Flake fish.

2. Separate yolk from white of egg.

3. Mix all ingredients well except egg white.

4. Beat white stiffly and fold in.

5. Put into well-greased mould.

6. Cover with greased paper.

7. Steam 15 minutes.

8. Turn onto a hot dish.

9. Garnish with lemon and parsley.

METHOD—MICROWAVE

1. Follow Conventional

Method 1–4.

2. Place in muffin pans.

3. Cook on HIGH for 6 minutes or until a firm shape.

4. Follow Conventional Method 8–9.

Serves 2

SMOKED FISH

INGREDIENTS

250 g haddock or cod
Juice of 1 lemon
1 blade mace (optional)
1 teaspoon butter
1 cup melted butter
sauce (see p. 224)

METHOD—CONVENTIONAL

1. Cut fish into suitably sized pieces.

2. Place in a pan or saucepan, cover with cold water, bring to boil, and simmer for 5 minutes.

3. Drain off the water.

4. Squeeze the lemon juice over the fish, add mace and

a small piece of butter.

5. Cover closely and heat gently for 10 to 15 minutes.

6. Serve plain or with melted butter sauce.

7. Garnish with parsley.

METHOD—MICROWAVE

Follow Conventional Method but cook on HIGH for 2 minutes in a glass or china heat-resistant dish covered with a paper towel.

Serves 2

FISH FLAN

INGREDIENTS

FLAN BASE
250 g cheese-flavoured cracker biscuits
125 g melted butter or margarine

FILLING
500 g cooked fresh, smoked or canned fish, prawns, crab meat or a mixture of these.
1½ cups thick basic
white sauce (see p. 224)
Few drops anchovy or tabasco sauce or lemon juice
Seasoning to taste

METHOD

FLAN BASE
1. Crush biscuits finely.

2. Combine well with butter or margarine and reserve 2 tablespoons of mixture.

3. Press mixture into a 20 cm well-greased flan or spring-form pan.

4. Bake base on the middle shelf of a moderate oven, 180°C, for 10 minutes.

FILLING
1. Combine sauce, fish, seasonings and flavourings.

2. Place in cooked base.

3. Sprinkle reserved crumbs on top.

4. Return to oven and bake to reheat and brown crumbs—approximately 15 minutes.

5. Garnish with lemon and parsley.

Serves 4

FISH CAKES

INGREDIENTS

4 medium potatoes, boiled
500 g cooked or canned fish
Salt and pepper to taste
1½ tablespoons butter
Little grated lemon rind
1 tablespoon chopped parsley
2 eggs
1 tablespoon flour
Breadcrumbs
Fat for frying

METHOD—CONVENTIONAL

1. Mash potatoes finely.

2. Break up fish, removing bones.

3. Mix together, and add salt, pepper, butter, lemon rind, parsley and 1 well-beaten egg.

4. Take small amounts of mixture and form into shapes.

5. Roll in flour then in beaten egg.

6. Coat well with breadcrumbs.

7. Fry for 3 minutes in a small amount of hot fat or

oil until a golden brown colour.

8. Drain on absorbent paper.

9. Serve on a hot dish.

10. Garnish with lemon wedges and sprigs of parsley.

METHOD—MICROWAVE

1. Follow above Method 1–6.

2. Place in muffin pans.

3. Cook on HIGH for 6 minutes or until a firm shape.

4. Follow Conventional Method 8–9.

Note: A large can of salmon, tuna or mackerel may be used instead of fresh fish.

Serves 6

SEAFOOD COCKTAIL

INGREDIENTS

Usually shellfish such as oysters, prawns, lobster meat,

crab meat and very lightly simmered and chilled scallops.

SAUCE

1 cup tomato sauce
6 tablespoons lemon juice
⅛ teaspoon salt
½ teaspoon celery salt
3 drops tabasco sauce or 1 teaspoon Worcestershire sauce
1 cup whipped cream or mayonnaise

METHOD

Combine the ingredients in the order listed. Bottle. Keep cold.

SERVING

Line a glass cocktail dish with lettuce, into this place a serving of cooked shelled prawns, or diced lobster meat or diced crab meat or a selected combination of any or all of the fish. Cover with 1 tablespoon of the sauce. Garnish with parsley and a wedge of lemon.

Oysters can be served on half the shell, placed around a small bowl or sauce for dipping, on a plate of ice. Garnish with lemon and parsley.

FISH KEDGEREE

INGREDIENTS

250 g cold cooked or canned fish
2 hard-cooked eggs
¼ cup rice
1 tablespoon butter
Chopped parsley
Salt and pepper to taste
Lemon juice
¼ cup milk

METHOD—CONVENTIONAL

1. Skin, bone and flake fish.

2. Remove yolks from eggs; chop whites.

3. Boil rice until tender; drain and keep hot.

4. Melt butter in saucepan.

5. Add chopped eggwhite, fish, parsley, salt and pepper, lemon juice and milk. Heat well.

6. Arrange heated rice on hot dish.

7. Place fish on top of rice.

8. Rub egg yolks through strainer and sprinkle over fish.

9. Garnish with lemon and sprigs of parsley.

METHOD—MICROWAVE

Follow Conventional Method but cook on HIGH until heated through in a glass or china heat-resistant dish covered with a paper towel.

Serves 2

SALMON AND MACARONI

INGREDIENTS

1½ cups macaroni or other type pasta
1 diced onion
1 can (440 g) salmon, tuna or smoked fish
2 tablespoons butter or margarine
2 tablespoons flour
2 cups milk
1 sliced tomato
2 tablespoons grated cheese

METHOD

1. Boil the macaroni and onion in salted water until tender.

2. Drain well and mix with fish.

3. Place in greased casserole dish.

4. Melt butter or margarine.

5. Stir in flour.

6. Add milk and stir until boiling.

7. Pour sauce over fish and macaroni.

8. Top with tomato and cheese.

9. Bake in a moderate oven, 180–200°C, until brown—about 10 minutes.

10. Garnish with lemon and parsley.

Serves 6

MEAT AND POULTRY DISHES

ABERDEEN SAUSAGE

INGREDIENTS

*500 g minced bladebone or
round or topside or chuck or
skirt steak
250 g fat bacon, rind removed
1 cup fresh breadcrumbs
¼ teaspoon salt
Pinch pepper
1 egg
1 tablespoon tomato sauce
1 tablespoon Worcestershire
sauce
½ cup brown breadcrumbs for
rolling*

METHOD

1. Have boiling water in
readiness.

2. Mince, grind or place
meat and bacon through a
food processor, add
breadcrumbs, salt and
pepper.

3. Beat the egg, add to it
the two sauces, and mix
with the other ingredients.

4. Press into a roll like a
thick sausage; tie it up in a
floured pudding cloth for
boiling, or in aluminium foil
for steaming.

5. Boil or steam for 2¼
hours; leave until cold, then
roll in breadcrumbs.

6. Serve cold, sliced thinly,
and garnished with
gherkins, cherry tomatoes,
parsley or watercress.

Serves 6

GRILLED BACON ROLLS

INGREDIENTS

4 bacon rashers, thinly sliced

METHOD

1. Cut rind off bacon, and cut bacon into 5 cm lengths.

2. Roll and thread loosely on a skewer.

3. Grill gently until fat is clear, about 5 minutes.

CORNED BEEF

INGREDIENTS

1 thick piece corned beef
1 teaspoon vinegar
6 cloves
12 peppercorns
1 teaspoon brown sugar
1 blade mace or 1 bay leaf
Carrots
Turnips

METHOD

1. Wash the meat.

2. Weigh, and allow at least 40 minutes' cooking time for each 500 g.

3. Place the meat in a saucepan of warm water with flavourings and vinegar and bring to simmering point.

4. Carrots and turnips may be cooked in the water with the meat: 30 minutes.

5. Serve on a hot plate with parsley, mustard, or onion sauce as an accompaniment (see p. 225).

Note: A pressure cooker can be used for corned beef to reduce cooking time.

LAMBS' BRAINS

INGREDIENTS

2 sets brains
1 small piece onion
2 sage leaves
Salt to taste

METHOD

1. Wash brains and remove skin.

2. Put in saucepan with

onion, sage and salt.

3. Cover with cold water, bring slowly to simmering point and simmer gently for 6 minutes and strain.

4. Use as required.

VARIATIONS

FRICASSEED   Cut cooked brains into 1 cm squares, add to 1⅓ cups hot medium basic white sauce (see p. 224). Reheat, add 1 teaspoon of chopped parsley and serve on a hot plate garnished with small triangles of dry toast.

SCALLOPED   Cut cooked brains into 1 cm squares, add to 1 cup masking sauce (see p. 224) with a squeeze of lemon juice and a little salt and cayenne pepper. Place mixture in scallop dish, greased and sprinkled thickly with dry breadcrumbs. Cover with crumbs and put small pieces of butter on top. Brown under griller or in moderate oven. Serve with sprigs of parsley and thin slices or rolls of bread and butter.

CAKES   Add mashed cooked brains to ⅔ cup panada (see p. 224) with a little salt, cayenne and grated nutmeg. Turn onto a plate and cool in the refrigerator. Form brain mixture into small round shapes in seasoned flour, dip in egg glazing and then in breadcrumbs, making them firm with a knife. Heat fat or oil and shallow-fry until golden brown. Drain on absorbent paper and serve on a hot plate garnished with small sprigs of parsley.

FRIED WITH BACON   Allow cooked brains to cool and cut each set into four. Roll brains in seasoned flour, brush with egg, toss in breadcrumbs, press crumbs on firmly with knife. Heat fat or oil and shallow-fry for 1 minute on each side, then cook gently for 3 minutes on each side. Drain on absorbent paper. Serve on a hot plate with bacon rolls and garnished with sprigs of parsley.

Serves 2

31

CHICKEN OR RABBIT PIE

INGREDIENTS

1 chicken or rabbit
2 tablespoons plain flour
½ teaspoon salt
Pinch pepper
1 onion
2 cups stock or water
2 sliced hard-cooked eggs
2 slices bacon, rind removed
2 tablespoons chopped parsley
1½ quantities flaky or
shortcrust pastry (see pp. 149, 150)

METHOD

1. Wash chicken or rabbit thoroughly and cut into neat joints.

2. Mix together the flour, salt and pepper on a plate.

3. Roll joints in seasoned flour.

4. Place in saucepan with onion; add stock or water and simmer 1½ hours or until tender.

5. Turn into pie dish to cool. Add hard-cooked eggs, bacon and parsley.

6. Roll out pastry in the shape of the pie dish with 2.5 cm extra all round.

7. Cut a narrow strip from the edge of the pastry, and lay it on the wet rim of the pie dish with the cut edge outside.

8. Brush with milk.

9. Place the remainder of the pastry over the top of the pie, making sure the narrow strip on the pie dish is completely covered.

10. Trim the edges with a sharp knife.

11. Ornament the top with a rose and leaves cut from the pastry leftovers.

12. Glaze by brushing with milk or yolk of egg.

13. Bake in hot oven, 220–250°C, for 20 minutes.

Serves 4–6

HARICOT CHOPS OR STEAK

INGREDIENTS

*500 g neck chops or round or
bladebone steak
1 medium-sized onion
1 tablespoon clarified fat or
oil
3 tablespoons plain flour
½ teaspoon salt
Pinch pepper
1¼ cups water or stock
1 carrot
1 turnip
1 stick celery
1 tablespoon parsley*

METHOD

1. Trim meat and remove excess fat.

2. Peel onion; slice into rings, or dice.

3. Melt fat or oil in saucepan. Brown meat, and remove from saucepan; brown onion and remove from saucepan.

4. Add flour, salt and pepper; allow to brown.

5. Add water and stir until simmering.

6. Add meat and onion and simmer gently for 1 hour.

7. Prepare vegetables, cut into rings or large dice.

8. Add vegetables and simmer all gently 1 hour longer.

9. Serve on a hot plate and sprinkle with chopped parsley.

Serves 4

GRILLED CHOPS OR FRENCH CUTLETS

INGREDIENTS

*Thick short loin chops or
cutlets, 2 per person*

METHOD

1. Remove skin (but not the fat) from chops.

2. Make into neat shapes and fasten with toothpicks.

3. Grill under moderate heat and allow to cook from 10 to 15 minutes, turning frequently.

4. Remove toothpicks and serve at once on a hot dish.

BEEF OLIVES

INGREDIENTS

*500 g thinly sliced round or
topside steak
4 tablespoons breadcrumbs
2 teaspoons chopped parsley
1 teaspoon each chopped
thyme and marjoram
¼ teaspoon salt
Pinch pepper
1 tablespoon butter,
chopped suet, or
clarified fat
Grated nutmeg
6 drops lemon juice
1 tablespoon fat or oil
1¼ cups water
2 tablespoons plain flour*

METHOD—CONVENTIONAL

1. Remove skin and fat
from steak.

2. Cut into pieces about
10 cm square and 1 cm
thick. Pound if desired.

3. Mix together
breadcrumbs, parsley,
thyme, marjoram, salt,
pepper, butter or suet,
nutmeg and lemon juice.

4. Place a little mixture on

each piece of steak, roll
steak up and tie firmly with
white string or cotton or
fasten with toothpicks.

5. Heat fat or oil in a
saucepan, and fry rolls of
meat until browned; pour
fat or oil away.

6. Add water to saucepan,
simmer very gently until
tender—approximately 1
hour.

7. Take out olives, remove
string or toothpicks

8. Blend flour with a little
cold water, add it to the
meat juices, stir until
boiling, and simmer gently
for 5 minutes. Replace the
olives and serve with the
gravy on a hot dish.

9. Dish may be
accompanied by mashed
potato, button squash,
carrots.

Note: Pan juices may be
reduced by rapid boiling in
uncovered saucepan instead of
thickening with flour. Veal,
pork or chicken can be
substituted for beef.

METHOD—MICROWAVE

1. Substitute ½ cup tomato puree for fat or oil, water and plain flour in the Conventional Method.

2. Follow Conventional Method 1–4.

3. Put rolls into a microwave-proof dish, top with tomato puree, cover with a glass lid or microwave-safe plastic wrap.

4. Microwave on HIGH for 5 minutes, MEDIUM for 12 minutes. Remove cover halfway through cooking and turn rolls.

5. Remove rolls from oven, let stand for 5 minutes covered with foil shiny side down.

6. Serve hot with tomato sauce and sprinkled with parsley.

Serves 4

GOULASH

INGREDIENTS

500 g round or topside steak
1 tablespoon plain flour
1 medium onion
1 tablespoon butter
1 cup stock or tomato puree
1 small clove garlic
1 teaspoon paprika
¼ teaspoon salt
Pinch pepper
1 potato

METHOD

1. Cut meat into cubes and roll in flour.

2. Peel and slice onion.

3. Lightly brown onion in melted butter. Add steak and brown.

4. Add stock or puree, and all other ingredients except potato.

5. Cover and simmer for about 1½ hours.

6. Cut potato into cubes and place on steak. Simmer another 20 to 30 minutes, or until potato is cooked.

7. Serve on hot plates.

Serves 4

DRY CURRY

INGREDIENTS

1 apple
1 onion
2 tablespoons butter or
substitute
½ tablespoon curry powder
500 g tender steak or veal or
equivalent in cooked meat
1 tablespoon chutney
1 tablespoon jam
1 sliced banana
2 tablespoons desiccated
coconut
1 tablespoon sultanas
1 tablespoon lemon juice
¼ teaspoon salt

METHOD

1. Cut the apple and onion
into dice.

2. Place in a saucepan with
the butter and curry
powder.

3. Fry without browning
for 10 minutes.

4. Cut the meat into small
dice; add to saucepan with
the chutney, jam, banana,
coconut and sultanas.

5. Simmer very gently for
about 1 hour or until the

meat is tender. If cooked
meat is used simmer gently
for 30 minutes.

6. Half an hour before
serving add the lemon juice
and salt.

7. Serve with boiled rice
(see p. 8).

Serves 4

CURRIED CHOPS,
STEAK OR CHICKEN

INGREDIENTS

750 g neck chops or round or
bladebone steak or chicken
pieces
1 onion
2 tomatoes
1 tablespoon oil
2 cloves garlic, chopped
Small knob green ginger, finely
chopped
1 tablespoon curry powder
¼ teaspoon salt
1 tablespoon vinegar

METHOD

1. Wipe meat with a damp
cloth.

2. Remove skin and excess
fat.

3. Prepare onion, and mince finely.

4. Pour boiling water over tomatoes in a bowl to remove skins.

5. Heat oil and fry garlic, onion and ginger until golden.

6. Add curry powder and salt and cook 1 minute.

7. Add vinegar and peeled, diced tomatoes.

8. Add meat and stir well until meat is coated, simmer 1½ hours.

9. Serve on a hot dish with a border of rice and slices of lemon.

10. Garnish with parsley.

Serves 6

IRISH STEW

INGREDIENTS

4 neck chops
2 tablespoons flour
¼ teaspoon salt
Pinch pepper
1¼ cups water
4 potatoes
1 onion

METHOD

1. Wipe chops with a damp cloth, and remove skin, gristle and fat.

2. Mix flour, salt and pepper on a plate.

3. Dip each chop in seasoned flour.

4. Place a little water in a saucepan and pack chops into it. Sprinkle any remaining seasoned flour over the chops, add the remainder of the water and bring quickly to simmering point.

5. Cook gently for 45 minutes.

6. Cut potatoes into pieces about 5 cm square, or rings 2.5 cm thick; slice onions into thin rings.

7. Place onions on meat, potatoes on top; allow to simmer gently 1 hour longer.

8. Serve on a hot plate, first lifting potatoes out, then chops. Pour gravy over.

Serves 4

FRICASSEED LAMB, CHICKEN OR RABBIT

INGREDIENTS

250 g neck chops or chicken or rabbit
1 small onion
¼ teaspoon salt
Pinch pepper
1 tablespoon plain flour
⅓ cup milk

METHOD

1. Wipe meat with a damp cloth.

2. Trim fat and marrow from chops, keeping a neat shape.

3. Dice onion.

4. Put meat and onion into a saucepan with sufficient water to barely cover them.

5. Add salt and pepper, bring to the boil, then simmer gently for 1½ hours.

6. Blend flour smoothly with a little milk.

7. Remove meat and onion from saucepan and measure liquid.

8. Return ⅓ cup of liquid to saucepan and add remaining milk.

9. Stir blended flour in carefully, return meat and onion to saucepan, and cook 3 minutes.

10. Serve on a hot dish, and garnish with parsley.

Serves 2

CORNISH PASTIES

INGREDIENTS

500 g round (or minced) steak
1 large potato
1 large onion
1 tablespoon chopped parsley
1 teaspoon salt
Pinch pepper
Double quantity shortcrust pastry (see p. 150)
Egg or milk for glazing

METHOD

1. Dice meat.

2. Peel potato and onion, wash and wipe dry, and dice.

3. Mix together the meat, potato, and onion with

parsley, salt and pepper.

4. Divide into 6 or 8 equal parts.

5. Heat the oven to 220–260°C.

6. Knead shortcrust until smooth.

7. Cut into 6 or 8 even pieces, and roll out each piece into a circle.

8. Place one heap of the meat and vegetable mixture on each piece of pastry.

9. Wet edges of pastry halfway round with water.

10. Turn into a half-moon shape, and join pastry edges together by pinching a small neat frill.

11. Place on a flat tin.

12. Glaze with egg or milk.

13. Bake in a hot oven, 220–260°C, for 10 minutes, and then reduce heat to 120–160°C, for 20 minutes longer.

14. Serve garnished with sprigs of parsley, and accompanied by tomato or plain brown sauce (see pp. 230, 226).

Makes 6–8

CROWN ROAST OF LAMB

INGREDIENTS

12–16 rib chops prepared by butcher for a crown roast (prepared as for cutlets but left in one piece), 2 ribs per serve.

METHOD

1. Form chops into a circle and tie securely.

2. Place in a greased baking dish.

3. Cover chop ends with greaseproof paper or aluminium foil to prevent burning.

4. Bake in a moderate oven, 180–200°C, allowing 20 minutes for each 500 g.

5. Serve on a hot plate.

Note: The centre of the crown may be partly filled with stuffing before cooking or, if the roast is to be served at table, cooked vegetables such as green peas and diced carrots may be placed in the centre.

CRUMBED FRIED CUTLETS

INGREDIENTS

6 cutlets
2 tablespoons plain flour
¼ teaspoon salt
Pinch pepper
1 egg
1 tablespoon milk
1 cup breadcrumbs
Enough fat or oil to cover
bottom of pan when melted

METHOD

1. Remove skin and gristle from cutlets and trim nicely, leaving about 5 cm of bare bone.

2. Mix flour, salt and pepper on a plate.

3. Beat egg on a plate. Add milk.

4. Spread breadcrumbs on white paper.

5. Dip cutlets in seasoned flour, brush with beaten egg and milk, and toss in breadcrumbs, pressing them on firmly with a knife.

6. Heat fat or oil, add cutlets, fry gently for 1 minute on each side, then cook gently for 10 to 15 minutes, turning once.

7. Drain cutlets on absorbent paper.

8. Have ready a mound of mashed potatoes on a hot plate, and place cutlets around it with the bones pointing upwards.

9. Serve with plain brown, tomato, or onion sauce (see pp. 226, 230, 225).

Serves 3

BONED SHOULDER OF LAMB OR MUTTON

INGREDIENTS

1 shoulder of lamb or mutton (boned)

STUFFING
1 cup fresh breadcrumbs
1 tablespoon butter or finely chopped suet
¼ teaspoon salt
Pinch pepper
1 tablespoon chopped parsley

*½ teaspoon each chopped
thyme and chopped marjoram
(or pinch dried herbs)
A little grated nutmeg or
lemon rind
1 egg or 2 tablespoons milk*

METHOD

1. Wipe meat with damp cloth and trim it.

2. Mix all stuffing ingredients together and moisten with egg or milk.

3. Fill meat with stuffing and sew up or tie.

4. Weigh joint and allow 30 minutes' cooking time for each 500 g.

5. Place in baking dish fat side up (if very lean add 1 or 2 tablespoons of fat or cooking oil).

6. Place in moderate oven, 180–200°C, and cook slowly for required length of time.

7. Make stock for gravy by simmering bone in 1¼ cups water.

8. Turn meat when half cooked.

9. Vegetables such as potatoes or pumpkin may be baked with meat. Allow from ¾ to 1 hour for these to cook.

10. When meat and vegetables are done, lift meat onto a hot serving dish and remove cotton used for sewing or string.

11. Drain vegetables on absorbent paper.

12. Keep hot while making thin brown gravy, and serve.

THIN BROWN GRAVY
Pour almost all the fat from the baking dish, sprinkle in 2 teaspoons plain flour, and allow to brown; add ⅔ cup stock (made from bone out of shoulder), and stir until boiling.

MEAT LOAF

INGREDIENTS

1 cup soft breadcrumbs
750 g minced topside steak
2 finely chopped onions
1 cup grated carrot
2 level tablespoons finely chopped parsley
1 teaspoon oregano
1 tablespoon Worcestershire sauce
2 tablespoons tomato sauce
1 level teaspoon salt
¼ level teaspoon pepper
1 egg

METHOD—CONVENTIONAL

1. Combine all ingredients well.

2. Press mixture into a well-greased and crumbed 20 cm × 8 cm loaf tin.

3. Bake in moderate oven, 200°C, for 1 to 1½ hours.

4. Cut into slices while hot, serve with vegetables or chill and serve with salad.

METHOD—MICROWAVE

Follow method as above but place in a microwave-safe loaf dish covered with greased paper and cook on HIGH for 15 minutes. Cover with foil and stand for 10 minutes before serving hot.

Serves 8

LIVER AND BACON

INGREDIENTS

1 lamb's fry
2 tablespoons flour
¼ teaspoon salt
Pinch pepper
Enough fat or oil to cover bottom of pan when melted
250 g fat bacon
2 cups water

METHOD

1. Wash liver well.

2. Dry liver and cut downwards in slices about 1 cm thick.

3. Mix flour, salt and pepper on a plate; coat each slice of liver in seasoned flour.

4. Heat fat or oil in frying pan.

5. Fry slices of liver slowly for 8 to 10 minutes, turning frequently.

6. Remove liver, drain on absorbent paper, and pour nearly all the fat or oil out of frying pan.

7. Cook bacon, remove, and keep hot.

8. Sprinkle remainder of seasoned flour into frying pan. Stir well until browned, add water, and stir until boiling.

9. Strain gravy if necessary and return to pan; add fried liver, and simmer gently from 7 to 10 minutes.

10. Serve liver and gravy on a hot plate, and garnish with bacon and chopped parsley.

Note: For Kidney and Bacon, use 6 lambs' or 4 pigs' kidneys and 2 rashers of bacon.

Serves 4

SIMMERED MUTTON, PUMPED OR SMOKED LEG

METHOD

1. Place a saucepan of water on to boil.

2. Trim mutton if necessary.

3. Weigh meat, and allow at least 30 minutes' cooking time for each 500 g.

4. Place thick side downward in the saucepan.

5. Simmer gently until tender. (Carrots and turnips may be boiled with it, cooking them for about ¾ hour.)

6. Serve on a hot dish accompanied by parsley, onion, or caper sauce (see p. 225).

7. If fresh meat has been used—when the water is cold, remove fat from top. This liquid may then be used in the making of broths and gravies.

POT ROAST

INGREDIENTS

*1 family sized piece of meat
(beef, lamb, mutton or poultry)
2 tablespoons plain flour
¼ teaspoon salt
Pinch pepper
Vegetables
Enough fat or oil to cover the
bottom of saucepan when
melted*

METHOD

1. Choose a heavy saucepan large enough to hold meat and vegetables.

2. Weigh meat and allow 30 minutes' cooking time for each 500 g.

3. Mix flour, salt and pepper, and rub well over meat.

4. Prepare vegetables.

5. Melt fat or oil in saucepan.

6. Brown meat. Remove from saucepan.

7. Brown vegetables. Remove.

8. Return meat to saucepan,

and cover with a tightly fitting lid.

9. Cook gently for the required time.

10. Return vegetables to saucepan, placing them around the meat, 40 minutes before serving time.

11. Drain on absorbent paper and serve on a hot plate.

12. Serve accompaniments as for Baked Meat (p. 51).

GRILLED STEAK

INGREDIENTS

Rump, fillet, sirloin, or T-bone steak

METHOD

1. Grease the bars of gridiron to prevent meat from sticking.

2. Grill meat under moderate heat, turning every 3 minutes.

3. Cook for about 12 to 15 minutes, according to

individual taste and to thickness of meat.

4. Serve on a hot plate with parsley butter (green butter see p. 245) (or butter, pepper, and salt), and potato chips (see p. 66).

FRIED OR GRILLED SAUSAGES

INGREDIENTS

6 sausages
2 tablespoons plain flour
¼ teaspoon salt
Pinch pepper
Enough fat or oil to cover the bottom of pan when melted
1¼ cups water

METHOD 1

FRIED

1. Prick sausages with a fork.

2. Mix flour, salt and pepper on a plate.

3. Dip sausages in seasoned flour.

4. Heat fat or oil and fry sausages gently until browned, about 20 minutes, turning every 5 minutes.

5. Drain sausages on absorbent paper.

6. Pour nearly all the fat out of pan, add remaining seasoned flour, and stir until browned; add water and stir until boiling.

7. Serve sausages with strained gravy on a hot plate.

METHOD 2

GRILLED

1. Prick sausages with a fork.

2. Arrange on grill tray.

3. Place under heated griller.

4. Cook gently until browned, about 20 minutes, turning every 5 minutes.

5. Serve on a hot plate with vegetables.

Serves 3

SEA PIE

INGREDIENTS

500 g of blade or chuck steak
1 tablespoon flour
½ teaspoon salt
Pinch pepper
2½ cups water
1 teaspoon vinegar
1 small carrot
1 small turnip
1 small onion
1½ quantities suet crust, or scone dough (see pp. 152, 204)

METHOD

1. Cut steak into small pieces.

2. Mix flour, salt and pepper together, and roll the meat in it.

3. Put meat, water and vinegar in a saucepan, bring to simmering point, and simmer ½ hour.

4. Prepare vegetables and cut into dice; add to saucepan and allow all to simmer gently ½ hour.

5. Roll pastry or dough to the same size as the saucepan lid, place on meat, and cut an incision in the centre of the pastry. Put lid on saucepan and cook gently ½ hour longer.

6. Cut pastry or dough into triangular pieces, lift out of saucepan, and serve on a hot plate with meat and vegetables.

Serves 6

SHARP STEAK

INGREDIENTS

1 kg topside or round steak
2 tablespoons flour
A little grated nutmeg
1 tablespoon brown sugar
¼ teaspoon salt
A little cayenne pepper
1¼ cups water
1 tablespoon vinegar
1 tablespoon Worcestershire sauce
1 tablespoon mushroom ketchup or tomato sauce

METHOD

1. Trim steak and cut into six servings. Mix together flour, nutmeg, sugar, salt and cayenne pepper, and rub well into steak.

2. Place in a deep ovenproof dish or casserole; add water, vinegar and sauces.

3. Cover with another dish or a lid.

4. Place in oven and cook slowly for 2 hours at 120–160°C after it reaches simmering point.

5. Lift steak onto a very hot dish or serve from casserole.

6. Serve garnished with gherkins cut in strips and a few capers.

Serves 6

FRICASSEED TRIPE AND ONION

INGREDIENTS

500 g tripe
½ teaspoon salt
1 white onion
1 tablespoon flour
⅔ cup milk
1 tablespoon butter
1 tablespoon chopped parsley

METHOD

1. Wash the tripe (scrape the underside if necessary), and cut it into pieces 2 cm square.

2. Place in a saucepan, cover with cold water, and add salt and peeled onion.

3. Cook gently until tender, 20 to 30 minutes, with lid on saucepan.

4. Blend the flour with a little of the milk.

5. Drain liquid off tripe, leaving ⅔ cup in saucepan.

6. Remove the onion, chop, and return to saucepan.

7. Add remaining milk, and butter.

8. When nearly boiling, add blended flour and stir until boiling, then cook for 1 minute.

9. Add chopped parsley.

10. Serve on a hot plate.

Note: Rolls of grilled bacon (see p. 30) and sippets of dry toast may be used as a garnish.

Serves 4

STEAK AND KIDNEY PIE

INGREDIENTS

500 g steak
4 sheep's kidneys
4 tablespoons plain flour
½ teaspoon salt
Pinch pepper
2 tablespoons chopped onion
2 tablespoons chopped bacon
Double quantity flaky or shortcrust pastry (see pp. 149, 150)
Egg yolk or milk for glazing

METHOD

1. Cut steak into thin slices, about 5 cm square.

2. Wash and skin kidney and cut into small pieces.

3. Mix flour, salt and pepper on a plate and roll steak in it.

4. Place steak, kidney, bacon and onion in a saucepan; add just enough water to cover.

5. Cook gently for 1½ to 2 hours or until tender. Cool and place in a pie dish.

6. Roll pastry out in the shape of the pie dish, with 2.5 cm extra all round.

7. Wet the rim of the pie dish with cold water.

8. Cut a narrow strip from the edge of the pastry, and place it on the wet rim of the pie dish, turning the cut edge to the outside, as cut edges rise better.

9. Moisten the strip with water, and put the remainder of the pastry over the top of the pie, making sure the strip on the pie dish rim is completely covered.

10. Trim the edges with a sharp knife.

11. Ornament the top with a rose and leaves made from the pastry scraps.

12. Make 3 incisions in the pastry.

13. Glaze with yolk of egg or milk.

14. Bake in a hot oven, 220–250°C, until the pastry is brown, about 20 minutes.

Note: A double quantity scone dough (see p. 204) may be substituted for pastry.

1. Follow Method 1–5. Press scone dough to size of dish. Place on top of mixture so that it covers wet edge of pie dish. Cook as for pie.

2. Follow Method 1–4. Place scone dough, whole or in shapes, on top of stew, put lid on tightly and cook gently 20 minutes. Serve sprinkled with finely chopped parsley, on hot plates.

Serves 4–6

VIENNA SCHNITZEL

INGREDIENTS

500 g fillet of veal
2 lemons
¼ cup flour
¼ teaspoon salt
Pinch pepper
1 egg
½ cup white breadcrumbs
4 tablespoons melted butter or oil

METHOD

1. Beat meat slices with a meat mallet until half their original thickness.

2. Pour juice of 1 lemon over meat, and let stand for ½ hour, turning several times.

3. Coat meat with flour, salt and pepper, then with beaten egg, and roll in breadcrumbs. Press crumbs on firmly.

4. Melt butter or heat oil, and fry meat gently on each side until cooked—10 to 15 minutes.

5. Drain on absorbent paper.

6. Serve hot, garnished with wedges of the remaining lemon, and accompanied by hot potato salad and stir-fried cabbage, onion and carrot.

Serves 4

STEAK AND KIDNEY PUDDING

INGREDIENTS

500 g steak
4 sheep's kidneys
2 tablespoons chopped onion
2 tablespoons chopped bacon
2 tablespoons flour
1 dessertspoon chopped parsley
½ teaspoon salt
Pinch pepper
2 quantities suet crust (see p. 152)
½ cup water

METHOD

1. Remove fat from meat and cut into 1 cm squares.

2. Wash and skin the kidneys, and cut into small pieces.

3. Mix steak, kidneys, bacon, onion, flour, parsley, salt and pepper on a plate.

4. Put a large saucepan of water on to boil.

5. Knead and roll out two-thirds of the pastry, and line a greased pudding basin with it.

6. Fill with meat mixture, piling high in the middle; add water, and wet around edges of the pastry.

7. Knead and roll out remainder of pastry, lay across top of basin, and where pastry lining and top meet at rim, press edges together and pinch a frill.

8. Cover pastry with greased paper or aluminium foil.

9. Place in a steamer or in a saucepan with water reaching halfway up the sides of the basin, and steam for 2 ½ to 3 hours.

10. Remove covering from pudding.

11. Serve on a hot plate.

Serves 4–6

SIMMERED PRESSED TONGUE

INGREDIENTS

4 sheep's tongues or 1 ox tongue
3 cloves
1 blade mace (optional)

METHOD

1. Wash tongues well.

2. Place cloves and mace in saucepan with enough water to cover tongues, and bring to boil.

3. Add tongues.

4. Simmer gently for 2 to 3 hours or until tender.

5. Remove skins.

6. Serve hot with parsley sauce (see p. 225).

7. If to be served cold, press after removing skin.

Note: A pressure cooker can be used for cooking tongues to reduce cooking time.

Serves 4

ROAST OR BAKED POULTRY OR RABBIT

METHOD

1. Wash and dry bird or rabbit.

2. Fill with stuffing.

3. Fasten into a neat shape.

4. Place in a baking dish lined with foil, prepared paper or use an oven bag.

5. Bake in moderate oven (see chart p. xxviii for temperature and time).

6. Serve with accompaniments (see chart pp. xxviii–xxxi).

Note: STUFFING

1. Chicken or Rabbit—Stuffing (see p. 242)

2. Turkey—Forcemeat (see p. 243)

3. Duckling—Sage and Onion Seasoning (see p. 244)

ROAST OR BAKED BEEF, VEAL, LAMB, MUTTON OR PORK

METHOD

1. Wipe over with damp paper towel and weigh.

2. Place in a baking dish lined with foil, prepared paper or use an oven bag.

3. See charts for oven temperature, cooking time and traditional accompaniments.

CASSEROLED MEATBALLS

INGREDIENTS

375 g minced steak
125 g sausage mince
1 onion chopped
2 tablespoons flour
1 tablespoon gravy powder
1½ cups water
2 teaspoons Worcestershire sauce
2 potatoes

METHOD

1. Mix meats and onion.

2. Shape into balls, roll in flour mixed with gravy powder.

3. Place in greased casserole dish.

4. Mix water with sauce and pour over meatballs.

5. Peel and slice potatoes and place in casserole over meatballs.

6. Cook with lid on for 35 to 40 minutes in moderate oven, 180–200°C.

Serves 4

STEAK AND PINEAPPLE CASSEROLE

INGREDIENTS

1 425 g can pineapple pieces
2 tablespoons plain flour
¼ teaspoon salt
Pinch pepper
Pinch mixed spice
1 teaspoon mustard
750 g topside or round steak
1 onion
1 tablespoon oil, margarine or butter
2 tablespoons vinegar
1 tablespoon soy sauce

METHOD

1. Drain juice from pineapple pieces and set aside.

2. Combine flour, salt, pepper, spice and mustard.

3. Cut meat into pieces, roll in seasoned flour.

4. Peel and chop onion.

5. Melt oil, margarine or butter in pan. Brown the onion and place in casserole dish.

6. Brown meat; add pineapple pieces.

7. Mix pineapple juice with sauce and vinegar.

8. Put meat and pineapple pieces into casserole dish.

9. Add juice and sauces. Mix well.

10. Cover and cook in a moderate oven, 168–180°C, for 2 hours or until meat is tender.

Serves 6

CREAMED CHICKEN

INGREDIENTS

1 medium-sized chicken or chicken pieces, previously steamed or pressure cooked
125 g mushrooms
1 small red capsicum
1 small green capsicum
2 tablespoons butter or margarine
1½ tablespoons plain flour
1¼ cups milk
2 egg yolks

METHOD

1. Cut chicken into small pieces, discarding skin and bone.

2. Slice mushrooms and seeded capsicums and fry in 1 tablespoon of the butter or margarine until limp but not brown.

3. Remove mushrooms and capsicums from pan and set aside; leave butter or margarine in pan.

4. Add the remaining butter or margarine and stir over low heat until just melted.

5. Mix in flour until smooth, then blend in the milk.

6. Stir over moderate heat until it boils and thickens.

7. Mix egg yolks in a small basin with 1 tablespoon of the cooked sauce.

8. Stir egg mixture into remaining sauce, then add the chicken and vegetables. Taste and add salt and pepper as desired.

Serves 4 as a dinner, or fills 2 dozen small pastry or bread cases for a party.

CHICKEN CASSEROLE

INGREDIENTS

1 no. 12 chicken
2 tablespoons seasoned plain flour
4 tomatoes
1 capsicum
2 small onions
1½ cups apricot nectar

METHOD

1. Cut chicken into serving size pieces, coat with seasoned flour.

2. Prepare vegetables (peel tomatoes) and slice.

3. Arrange chicken and vegetables in layers in casserole dish.

4. Pour apricot nectar on top.

5. Bake in moderate oven for 45 minutes.

6. Serve sprinkled with parsley.

Vegetable accompaniments: baked jacket potato and a green vegetable.

Serves 4

SWEET AND SOUR PORK

INGREDIENTS

1 425 g can unsweetened pineapple pieces
500 g lean pork
1 tablespoon margarine, butter or oil
½ cup sliced carrots
½ cup chopped celery
1 large onion, chopped
½ cup chopped capsicum
Pepper to taste
¾ cup stock or water
2 tablespoons maize cornflour
1 tablespoon vinegar
1 tablespoon soy sauce
2 tablespoons brown sugar

METHOD

1. Strain juice from pineapple pieces.

2. Cut pork into bite-size pieces, and fry in margarine, butter or oil until meat changes colour.

3. Add carrots, celery, onions, capsicum and pepper.

4. Stir in stock and pineapple juice, cover the

pan and cook until pork is tender (approximately ½ to 1 hour).

5. Blend the cornflour with the vinegar, soy sauce and sugar.

6. Stir into pork and vegetable mixture.

7. Add pineapple pieces.

8. Cook over a slow heat until mixture boils.

9. Serve hot with boiled or fried rice.

Serves 6

SCOTCH EGG LOAF

INGREDIENTS

500 g (1¾ cups) hamburger mince
250 g (¾ cup) sausage mince
2 bacon rashers
1 cup fresh breadcrumbs
½ teaspoon salt
½ teaspoon pepper
1 egg
1 tablespoon tomato sauce
1 tablespoon Worcestershire sauce
3 hard-cooked eggs

METHOD

1. Grease loaf tin.

2. Place mince in basin.

3. Chop bacon finely; add to breadcrumbs, salt and pepper, and combine with mince.

4. Beat egg, add sauces, and mix well with other ingredients.

5. Put half the mixture into prepared tin.

6. Place the hard-cooked eggs down the centre lengthwise, and cover with the other half of mince mixture.

7. Bake in a moderate oven, 180–190°C, for about 1½ hours. The tin may be covered with greaseproof paper or foil for 1 hour, after which the paper or foil is removed to allow the meat to brown.

8. Serve hot with cooked vegetables or cold with salad.

Serves 4–6

PORK KEBABS

INGREDIENTS

¾ cup olive oil
2 tablespoons chopped mixed
fresh herbs
1 teaspoon paprika
1 kg lean pork cubes
2 capsicums
4 rashers bacon
4 cups cooked brown rice
2 tablespoons fresh chopped
parsley

METHOD

1. Mix olive oil, chopped, mixed fresh herbs and paprika, and pour over the pork cubes. Marinate 1 to 2 hours.

2. Remove seeds and slice capsicum in 2 cm rings.

3. Remove rind and cut bacon in 8 cm pieces.

4. Thread on a skewer a folded slice of capsicum, a folded piece of bacon, a pork piece, bacon and capsicum. Repeat twice.

5. Grill under medium heat until golden brown.

6. Serve hot on a bed of rice seasoned with chopped parsley.

Serves 6

MUSTARD PORK STEAKS

INGREDIENTS

4 midloin butterfly steaks
½ cup chopped onions
2 teaspoons prepared English
mustard
2 teaspoons brown sugar
1 clove garlic, crushed
1 tablespoon Worcestershire
sauce
120 ml dry sherry or orange
juice
1 cup canned tomatoes,
pureed
¼ teaspoon seasoned pepper

METHOD

1. Arrange steaks on a rack in a baking dish and bake in a moderate oven for 30 minutes.

2. Place remainder of ingredients in a saucepan and bring to the boil. Reduce heat and simmer until the sauce is reduced by half.

3. Pour sauce over the steaks.

4. Serve with a variety of cooked vegetables.

Serves 4

RISSOLES

INGREDIENTS

500 g minced topside or lean chuck steak
1 medium onion, finely chopped
1 cup soft breadcrumbs
1 egg well beaten and seasoned
½ teaspoon dried mixed herbs
1 tablespoon chopped parsley

METHOD

1. Blend all ingredients well together.

2. Shape into balls the size of a small apple. Make 8 or 12 if main meal. Make balls half size if serving as meatballs with pasta and tomato.

3. Coat each rissole well with flour. This may be done by putting flour in a bag then shaking two rissoles at a time in flour. Remove excess flour.

4. Shallow-fry for 20 minutes turning and browning on all sides.

5. A brown gravy (p. 225) can be made with pan drippings. Serve rissoles very hot with cooked vegetables.

Serves 4–6

STEWED CHOPS AND RICE

INGREDIENTS

2 neck chops
½ teaspoon salt
1 small onion
1¼ cups water
2 tablespoons rice

METHOD

1. Wipe chops and remove skin.

2. Put into a saucepan with salt and chopped onion.

3. Cover with water.

4. Bring to boil.

5. Simmer gently for ½ hour.

6. Sprinkle in the well-washed rice.

7. Simmer gently 1 hour longer, being careful that the rice does not stick or burn.

8. When cooked, lift chops onto a hot plate and pour the rice and gravy round them.

Serves 2

BOILED HAM

INGREDIENTS

1 ham
Cloves
Breadcrumbs

METHOD

1. Soak ham overnight in cold water in boiler.

2. Place large boiler of water on to heat.

3. When water is warm place ham in boiler. (Water must cover ham.)

4. Bring very slowly to the boil.

5. Cook very slowly until tender when tested with a skewer (about 60 minutes per kg).

6. Remove skin; sprinkle thickly with browned breadcrumbs and stick with cloves.

Note: Bacon may be treated in the same way, omitting the breadcrumbs and cloves. Ham may be boiled 1 hour, then covered with a thick packing of clean hessian or kitchen towels and allowed to stand 24 hours.

SATAY

INGREDIENTS

*300 g lean boned meat
(chicken, lamb, pork or beef)
2 teaspoons soy sauce
1 teaspoon honey
Pinch chilli powder
1 teaspoon cumin
2 tablespoons oil
Bamboo satay skewers soaked
in water for an hour or so*

METHOD

1. Slice meat into thin
strips.

2. Mix all other ingredients
and add meat, mix until
each piece of meat is
coated.

3. Leave for 30 minutes to
marinate.

4. Thread meat on skewers.

5. Grill on a foil-lined
griller, turn 2 or 3 times.

6. Serve with peanut sauce
(see p. 226).

*Serves 3 with rice, 6 as
snacks.*

VEGETABLES

BAKED VEGETABLES

Potato, pumpkin, sweet potato, onion and parsnip are suitable for baking.

METHOD

1. Prepare vegetables according to kind.
2. Dry thoroughly.
3. Put in baking dish with meat and cook for 40 to 45 minutes.
4. Turn once.
5. Drain on absorbent paper.
6. Serve hot.

ASPARAGUS

INGREDIENTS

1 bunch asparagus

METHOD

1. Wash and scrape each stick of asparagus, being careful not to break the tops.
2. Tie into bundles, keeping the tops together.
3. Place asparagus upright in saucepan.
4. Add enough boiling water to reach the base of the green tips.
5. Boil for 15 to 20 minutes, or until tender.
6. Remove carefully, drain.
7. Remove the string.
8. Serve hot with a bowl of

melted butter and lemon juice.

Alternative Method

1. Wash and trim.

2. Place one layer in an electric frypan.

3. Barely cover with cold water.

4. Bring to boil and cook for 10 minutes or until tender.

5. Serve hot, or chill and store in refrigerator.

BEANS

INGREDIENTS

500 g beans
Salt if desired
Pinch pepper

METHOD

1. Wash beans.

2. Cut off ends and strings from sides.

3. Slice or leave whole as preferred.

4. Place beans in saucepan and barely cover with

boiling water.

5. Boil for 2 minutes then place lid on saucepan, boil until tender—10 to 15 minutes.

6. Drain and serve on a hot dish.

Serves 4

BROAD BEANS

INGREDIENTS

500 g broad beans
Salt if desired
Butter or margarine

METHOD

1. Shell beans and wash.

2. Put beans in a saucepan, and barely cover with boiling water.

3. Boil for 2 minutes, then put lid on saucepan and boil for a further 10 to 20 minutes until tender.

4. Drain.

5. Place on a hot dish with a little butter.

6. Serve very hot.

Serves 4

CABBAGE
OR SPINACH

INGREDIENTS

1 cabbage or 1 bunch spinach
Salt if desired
2 tablespoons butter or
margarine
Pinch pepper

METHOD

1. Wash and slice cabbage or spinach.

2. Melt butter in a saucepan.

3. Add sliced vegetable.

4. Cover with a tightly fitting lid.

5. Simmer gently for 7 to 10 minutes or until tender. Shake saucepan occasionally but do not remove lid.

6. Drain thoroughly.

7. Serve hot, sprinkled with pepper.

Note: Cabbage may be lightly sprinkled with caraway seeds.

BOILED BEETROOT

METHOD

1. Cut tops off beetroot, leaving 15 cm of the stalk and the roots.

2. Wash thoroughly. Be careful not to scrape or cut.

3. Place beetroot in saucepan and cover with boiling water.

4. Boil with the lid on until tender.

5. Test if cooked (stalk will leave root easily).

6. Drain.

7. Remove skin.

8. Serve hot as a vegetable or use for pickling (see cold beetroot p. 71).

CARROTS
OR PARSNIPS

METHOD

1. Wash well.

2. Remove skins if desired. Cut as required.

3. Place in saucepan and

barely cover with boiling water.

4. Boil with the lid on until tender, from 10 to 15 minutes.

5. Drain.

6. Serve on a hot dish.

CAULIFLOWER OR BROCCOLI

METHOD

1. Cut away the thick stalk and outside leaves. Cut into serving sized pieces.

2. Wash well under tap or in salted water.

3. Place in saucepan and barely cover with boiling water.

4. Boil gently with lid on until tender—10 to 15 minutes.

5. Lift out carefully.

6. Place in a hot dish or plate.

Note: The vegetable may be served with basic white or cheese sauce (see pp. 224, 225).

MARROW, SQUASH OR ZUCCHINI

METHOD

1. Wash.

2. Cut into pieces or leave whole, as preferred.

3. Place in saucepan and barely cover with boiling water.

4. Boil with lid on until tender—10 to 15 minutes.

5. Lift out carefully or drain.

6. Serve on a hot dish or plate. Cover marrow or squash with a basic white masking sauce (see p. 224), and garnish with finely chopped parsley; serve zucchini with butter and pepper.

CELERY

METHOD

1. Separate celery, wash well.

2. Cut into pieces about 2 cm long.

3. Place in saucepan and barely cover with boiling water.

4. Boil gently with the lid on until tender—10 to 15 minutes.

5. Drain.

6. Place on a hot dish and cover with masking sauce (see p. 224), using celery liquid with milk.

CHOKOES OR JERUSALEM ARTICHOKES

METHOD

1. Wash well.

2. Peel if required.

3. Cut chokoes into halves or quarters; leave artichokes whole.

4. Place in saucepan and barely cover with boiling water.

5. Boil gently with lid on for 10 to 15 minutes or until tender.

6. Drain.

7. Serve on a hot dish or plate coated with masking sauce (see p. 224).

MASHED POTATOES

INGREDIENTS

4 medium-sized boiled potatoes (see p. 66)
2 teaspoons butter
2 tablespoons milk

METHOD

1. Mash potatoes in the saucepan using potato masher, fork or wooden spoon.

2. Add butter and milk.

3. Beat well.

4. Stir over stove to reheat.

5. Serve on a hot dish or plate.

Serves 4

ONIONS OR LEEKS

METHOD

1. Remove outer skins and wash.

2. Place in saucepan and barely cover with boiling water.

3. Boil for 2 minutes, then put lid on saucepan and boil for 20 minutes or until tender.

4. Drain.

5. Serve on a hot dish or plate with a basic white masking sauce (see p. 224).

mint and barely cover with boiling water.

3. Boil gently with lid on until tender—10 to 15 minutes.

4. Drain.

5. Remove mint.

6. Add butter and pepper.

7. Shake over heat.

8. Serve on a hot dish.

Note: Snow peas—remove stalk, boil for 3 minutes. Sugar peas—remove stalk and string, cook as for green peas.

Serves 4

GREEN PEAS

INGREDIENTS

500 g peas
3 sprigs mint
1 teaspoon butter
Pinch pepper

METHOD

1. Shell peas and wash.

2. Place in saucepan, add

SWEET CORN

METHOD

1. Remove husks.

2. Wash.

3. Place in a saucepan and cover with boiling water (no salt).

4. Boil gently for 8 to 12 minutes until tender.

5. Serve with butter.

BOILED POTATOES

METHOD

1. Wash potatoes.

2. Peel very thinly if necessary, remove the eyes, and cut into pieces of equal size.

3. Put in saucepan and barely cover with boiling water.

4. Boil gently with lid on until tender, about 15 to 20 minutes.

5. Test with a skewer; if soft on the outside and just a little firm in the centre, they are cooked.

6. Drain.

7. Serve whole or mashed (see p. 64).

POTATO CHIPS

METHOD

1. Wash, dry, and thinly peel potatoes.

2. Cut into thin strips or fancy shapes.

3. Thoroughly dry.

4. Half fill a saucepan with fat or oil, and heat slowly till a blue fume or haze rises.

5. Place potatoes in a frying basket, lower into fat, and cook for 2 to 3 minutes.

6. Lift out and allow fat or oil to become smoking hot.

7. Put chips into fat or oil again, and fry until golden brown.

8. Drain on absorbent paper, sprinkle with pepper and salt and serve.

SCALLOPED POTATOES

INGREDIENTS

1 teaspoon butter
2 medium-sized potatoes
1 onion
1 tablespoon flour
Salt and pepper
Milk
2 tablespoons grated cheese

METHOD

1. Grease an ovenproof dish with butter.

2. Peel and thinly slice potatoes and onion.

3. Pack in layers in dish, sprinkling each layer with a little flour and salt and pepper.

4. Pour in enough milk to just cover potato and onion.

5. Spread cheese on top.

6. Bake in a moderate oven for about 1 hour.

Serves 2

BOILED PUMPKIN

METHOD

1. Wash well.

2. Cut into pieces and remove the seeds.

3. Place in saucepan and barely cover with boiling water.

4. Boil with lid on for 15 to 20 minutes until tender.

5. Drain.

6. Serve whole, or mashed with butter and pepper, on a hot dish or plate.

BAKED JACKET POTATOES

METHOD

1. Wash, scrub and dry potatoes.

2. Remove eyes, prick skin.

3. Place on top shelf of oven and bake in a moderate oven for approximately 1 to 1¼ hours until tender.

Note: Serve plain or split and top with sour cream and chopped chives.

WHITE OR SWEDE TURNIPS

METHOD

1. Scrub.

2. Peel thickly and cut into suitable sizes.

3. Place in saucepan and barely cover with boiling water.

4. Boil until tender—15 to 20 minutes.

5. Drain.

6. Serve whole, or mashed with a little butter and pepper, on a hot dish or plate.

RATATOUILLE

INGREDIENTS

1 small eggplant (aubergine), cut into 1 cm pieces
Salt
2 tablespoons oil
1 chopped onion
1 clove garlic, crushed
2 large zucchini, thickly sliced
1 sliced red or green capsicum
3 medium tomatoes, peeled and chopped
¼ teaspoon oregano
Salt and pepper to taste

METHOD

1. Sprinkle eggplant with salt and stand for 30 minutes. Rinse and pat dry with paper towel.

2. Heat the oil in a saucepan. Saute the onion and garlic until soft but not brown.

3. Add the eggplant, zucchini, capsicum, tomatoes, oregano and salt and pepper.

4. Cover and simmer gently for 30 minutes.

Note: Ratatouille may be served hot or cold.

STIR-FRIED VEGETABLES

INGREDIENTS

A variety of vegetables may be used.
Root vegetables are thinly sliced or coarsely grated.

METHOD

1. Prepare vegetables as for boiling.

2. Heat a small amount of oil in a wok, frying pan or deep saucepan.

3. Put vegetables in oil, and stir lightly and quickly until cooked.

4. Serve as an accompaniment to any meat, fish or poultry dish.

SALADS AND SALAD DRESSINGS

Choice and Preparation of Vegetables for Salads

CAPSICUMS
*Wash, remove centre and seeds. Cut into rings,
slice or dice.*

CARROTS
Wash. Peel if old. Grate or slice finely.

CELERY
*Wash. Cut into suitable lengths or chop. To curl celery
for garnish, cut into 2 cm to 4 cm lengths, then from
one end cut into strips to within 1 cm of the other end,
and soak in cold or iced water.*

CUCUMBER
Wash. Peel or score if required. Slice thinly.

LETTUCE
Remove core and coarse outer leaves, wash, drain.

MUSHROOMS
*Trim stalks, brush with soft pastry brush or wipe over
with paper towel.*

RADISHES
*Wash. Remove roots and leaves. Cut into shapes or
leave whole.*

SHALLOT AND SPRING ONION
Remove root and outer layer and portion of green top. Wash and drain.

TOMATOES
Wash. Remove skins if preferred. Slice or cut into wedges.

Individual or side salads can be prepared by arranging small salads in lettuce leaves.

GREEN SALAD

INGREDIENTS

Crisp lettuce
Cucumber
Green capsicum
Onion or shallots
Avocado if liked
Celery
French dressing (see p. 72).
Watercress

METHOD

1. Wash and prepare vegetables.

2. Dry lettuce thoroughly and tear with fingers.

3. Slice or dice cucumber, capsicum, onion and avocado.

4. Curl celery (see p. 69).

5. Tumble all vegetables in bowl with French dressing.

6. Garnish with sprigs of watercress.

COLESLAW

INGREDIENTS

¼ of a young cabbage
1 capsicum
1 apple
1 carrot
1 tablespoon chives or 1 onion
Stick celery
Salt and pepper to taste
Salad dressing 2 (see p. 72)

METHOD

1. Wash and dry cabbage.

2. Shred finely and place in a bowl.

3. Chop or grate other vegetables and fruit and mix with cabbage.

4. Add salt and pepper.

5. Pour dressing over vegetables and mix lightly.

COLD BEETROOT

INGREDIENTS

⅔ *cup vinegar*
3 cloves
1 blade mace (optional)
1 teaspoon salt
1 tablespoon sugar
6 peppercorns
1 bunch cooked beetroot (see p. 62)

METHOD

1. Put vinegar, cloves, mace, salt, sugar and peppercorns in a saucepan.

2. Bring to the boil and simmer for 3 minutes.

3. Strain and stand aside until cool.

4. Peel beetroot and slice.

5. Place sliced beetroot in a bowl and pour liquid over it.

HARD-COOKED EGGS FOR SALADS, ETC.

METHOD

1. Place eggs in boiling water, unless taken from the refrigerator, in which case place in cold water and bring to boil.

2. Allow to simmer gently for 15 to 20 minutes.

3. Lift out and stand in a basin of cold water to prevent eggs from discolouring.

4. Change water as it becomes warm.

SALAD DRESSING 1

INGREDIENTS

1 yolk hard-cooked egg
¼ teaspoon mustard
2 teaspoons sugar
½ teaspoon salt
1 teaspoon salad oil or melted butter
3 tablespoons milk or cream or 1 tablespoon condensed milk
3 tablespoons vinegar

METHOD

1. Pound the yolk of the egg in a basin with the back of a wooden spoon.

2. Add mustard, sugar and salt.

3. Work oil in gradually, very slowly add milk or cream, and vinegar last.

4. Serve in a small glass jug or pour over salad.

Note: When condensed milk is used instead of cream, omit the sugar.

SALAD DRESSING 2

INGREDIENTS

¼ teaspoon mustard
½ teaspoon salt
2 teaspoons sugar
1 tablespoon condensed milk
2 tablespoons milk
2 tablespoons vinegar

METHOD

1. Mix mustard, salt, sugar and condensed milk together in a small basin.

2. Add milk.

3. Stir in vinegar last, very gradually.

4. Serve in a small jug or pour onto salad.

FRENCH DRESSING

INGREDIENTS

3 tablespoons edible oil
1 tablespoon vinegar (plain or flavoured) or lemon juice
Salt and cayenne to taste

METHOD

1. Place oil in a container.

2. Add vinegar gradually, beating and shaking vigorously until smooth.

3. Season.

COOKED SALAD DRESSING

INGREDIENTS

2 tablespoons butter
1 egg
½ cup milk
½ cup sugar
½ teaspoon salt
1 teaspoon mustard
¼ cup vinegar

METHOD

1. Melt butter in a saucepan; remove from heat.

2. Add beaten egg and milk.

3. Add sugar, salt and mustard.

4. Add vinegar last.

5. Return to heat and stir until it coats the spoon, without boiling.

Note: This is better made in a double saucepan. It will keep for three weeks if chilled.

SALMON MAYONNAISE

INGREDIENTS

1 cucumber
Tomatoes or beetroot
1 lettuce
1 can (440 g) salmon
Salt and pepper to taste
1¼ cups mayonnaise (p. 74)
or salad dressing (p. 72)

METHOD

1. Prepare vegetables.

2. Arrange in bowl.

3. Place a portion of salmon on each lettuce leaf. Season with salt and pepper.

4. Mask salmon with mayonnaise (or the mayonnaise may be served separately in a small jug).

5. Garnish with radishes and celery curls.

Serves 2

MAYONNAISE

INGREDIENTS

2 egg yolks (raw)
½ teaspoon salt
Pinch pepper
¼ teaspoon mustard
6 tablespoons melted butter or
polyunsaturated oil
2 tablespoons tarragon
vinegar

METHOD

1. Place egg yolks, salt, pepper and mustard in a basin: mix well.

2. Add a few drops of oil or butter and work in very gradually with a wooden spoon.

3. Add a few drops of vinegar and work in very gradually. Continue slowly until all the oil and vinegar are added.

Note: The success of this recipe depends on the continuous beating, and on making the mayonnaise in a very cool place; in warm weather it is best to place the basin on ice while beating.

CAULIFLOWER SALAD

INGREDIENTS

1 small cauliflower
10 small white onions
1 300 ml carton sour cream
1 tablespoon mayonnaise
1 tablespoon chopped parsley
1 tablespoon chopped chives
1 tablespoon capers or
caraway seeds
Salt and pepper to taste

METHOD

1. Break the cauliflower into flowerets, drop into boiling salted water and boil for 5 minutes. Drain and place in cold water. When cool drain in a colander.

2. Remove skins from onions and cook as for cauliflower.

3. Combine sour cream, mayonnaise, parsley, chives, capers or caraway seeds, salt and pepper.

4. Place cauliflower and onions in a bowl and pour dressing over. Stir lightly and chill.

5. Place into serving dish.

MUSHROOM SALAD

INGREDIENTS

250 g button mushrooms
½ cup olive oil
2 tablespoons white wine vinegar
1 teaspoon sugar
1 teaspoon mustard powder
½ teaspoon salt
12 grinds fresh black pepper
2 cloves garlic, crushed
Chopped parsley for garnish

METHOD

1. Trim mushroom stalks.

2. Brush mushrooms with soft pastry brush or wipe over with paper towel.

3. Slice thinly and place in a shallow serving dish.

4. Place oil, vinegar, sugar, mustard powder, salt, pepper and garlic in a screw-top jar and shake well until evenly mixed.

5. Pour dressing over mushrooms.

6. Cover with clear plastic wrap.

7. Chill for 30 minutes.

8. Garnish salad with chopped parsley and serve.

POTATO SALAD

INGREDIENTS

150 ml cream
1 tablespoon of lemon juice or vinegar
500 g cooked diced potatoes
2 tablespoons chopped shallots or chives
2 tablespoons chopped parsley
1 tablespoon chopped mint

METHOD

1. Whip the cream, blend in lemon juice or vinegar, salt to taste and freshly ground black pepper.

2. Combine in a large bowl the other ingredients.

3. Mix the cream through, being careful not to break up potato cubes.

4. Chill before serving with other cold foods.

Note: Wash and boil potatoes in their skins which will peel off easily when cold.

POTATO AND BACON SALAD

INGREDIENTS

4 rashers lean bacon
1 ½ tablespoons flour
1 tablespoon chopped onion
⅓ cup vinegar
⅓ cup water
¼ cup sugar
Salt and freshly ground black pepper
1 teaspoon prepared German mustard
½ teaspoon caraway seeds (if liked)
500 g cooked diced potato
1 tablespoon chopped parsley

METHOD

1. Fry bacon until crisp. Remove from pan, drain and crumble.

2. Add flour and onion to the bacon fat in the pan. Stir well.

3. Stir in vinegar, water, sugar, salt, pepper, mustard and caraway seeds.

4. Cook until mixture is of a medium thickness.

5. Add to the potatoes, parsley and crumbled bacon in a large bowl. Mix carefully to prevent breaking potato cubes.

6. Serve hot with schnitzel or roast veal or cold with other cold foods.

RICE OR PASTA SALAD

INGREDIENTS

2 cups cold cooked rice or pasta
¼ cup chopped red or green capsicum
¼ cup sliced button mushrooms
¼ cup sliced celery
¼ cup sliced shallots
¼ cup corn kernels (drained)
Salt and pepper to taste
2 tablespoons edible oil
2 tablespoons vinegar
Lettuce leaves

METHOD

1. Place rice or pasta in a bowl.

2. Add capsicum,

mushrooms, celery, shallots, corn kernels, salt and pepper.

3. Place oil and vinegar in a jar with a screw top. Shake vigorously.

4. Pour oil and vinegar over combined ingredients and toss well. Chill.

5. Serve in a serving dish lined with washed and dried lettuce leaves.

6. Garnish with watercress or parsley.

TABBOULEH

INGREDIENTS

1 cup burghul (crushed wheat)
¾ cup finely chopped white onion
Salt and pepper to taste
1½ cups finely chopped Italian parsley
¾ cup finely chopped mint
½ cup lemon juice
½ cup olive oil
2 tomatoes peeled, seeded and finely chopped

METHOD

1. Soften burghul by soaking in water for 1–1½ hours, drain well on absorbent paper and press out excess water.

2. Mix burghul, onion, salt and pepper together crushing onion pieces into burghul with fingers.

3. Add parsley, mint, lemon juice, oil and tomato and mix thoroughly.

4. Add more lemon juice if necessary.

5. Serve on lettuce leaves in individual dishes, with Lebanese bread or on a large platter and decorate with sliced tomatoes.

Note: Non-fat yoghurt may be used instead of olive oil.

MIXED BEAN SALAD

INGREDIENTS

1 *450 g can mixed beans*
1 *cup boiled sliced green beans*
1 *small onion, finely chopped*
¼ *cup chopped red capsicum*
Salt and pepper to taste
¼ *cup edible oil*
¼ *cup white vinegar*

METHOD

1. Place beans, onion, capsicum, salt and pepper in a bowl.

2. Shake salad oil and vinegar in a screw-top jar.

3. Add oil and vinegar dressing to other ingredients and mix well.

4. Chill.

5. Place bean salad in a serving dish and garnish with parsley.

BARLEY SALAD

INGREDIENTS

¾ *cup pearl barley*
2 *tablespoons lemon juice*
1 *large onion, finely chopped*
6 *tablespoons salad oil*
Salt and pepper to taste
3 *large tomatoes, skinned and chopped*
½ *cup chopped parsley*
¼ *cup chopped mint*

METHOD

1. Soak barley in cold water overnight.

2. Drain barley, place in saucepan and cover with water. Bring to the boil and simmer 20 minutes or until tender. Drain.

3. Place barley in a bowl and add lemon juice, onion, oil, salt and pepper. Cover and chill.

4. Add tomatoes, parsley and mint. Chill well.

5. Place in serving dish.

COLD MEAT COOKERY

CURRY AND RICE

INGREDIENTS

250 g cooked meat
1 apple
1 onion
1 tablespoon fat or oil
1 tablespoon sultanas
½ teaspoon salt
2 teaspoons curry powder
1 tablespoon plain flour
1 cup stock or water
1 teaspoon lemon juice
½ cup boiled rice (see p. 8)
1 pinch pepper

METHOD

1. Cut meat into small pieces, removing all fat and gristle.

2. Cut apple and onion into dice.

3. Heat fat or oil in a saucepan.

4. Fry the onion and apple.

5. Add all the dry ingredients except meat and rice, and stir for 1 minute over heat.

6. Add water or stock and stir until boiling.

7. Simmer gently for 15 minutes.

8. Add the meat and lemon juice and allow to simmer in the sauce until the meat is thoroughly heated, about 10 minutes.

9. Serve on a hot plate, and arrange rice round the curry and garnish with thin half slices of lemon, standing the lemon up.

10. Grate the yolk of a hard-cooked egg over the rice, or sprinkle with chopped parsley.

Serves 4

COLD MEAT FRITTERS

INGREDIENTS

350 g any leftover cooked meat
1 tablespoon chopped parsley
½ teaspoon salt
Pinch pepper
1 cup self-raising flour (white or wholemeal)
1 egg
½ cup milk
A little lemon juice
Oil

METHOD

1. Dice meat.

2. Place into a bowl with parsley, salt, pepper and flour.

3. Beat egg, combine with milk and lemon juice, and blend into the dry mixture to form a dropping consistency.

4. Heat sufficient oil to cover the surface of the pan.

5. Drop 1 tablespoon of meat mixture into the oil and allow to brown. Turn.

6. Cook until brown.

7. Drain on absorbent paper.

8. Serve on a hot plate garnished with parsley.

Serves 4

SHEPHERD'S PIE

INGREDIENTS

250 g cooked meat
¼ teaspoon mixed dried herbs
1 tablespoon chopped parsley
1 tablespoon plain flour
¼ teaspoon salt
Pinch pepper
A little grated lemon rind or nutmeg (optional)
½ cup stock or water
4 medium-sized cold cooked potatoes
A little butter and milk

METHOD

1. Chop the meat finely, removing skin and gristle.

2. Put in a saucepan with herbs, parsley, flour, salt, pepper, lemon rind or nutmeg, and stock or water, and stir over heat for 5 minutes or until it thickens and leaves the side of the saucepan.

3. Mash the potatoes, adding a little butter and milk to make them smooth.

4. Grease a pie dish.

5. Line pie dish with a thin layer of mashed potato.

6. Add the meat mixture.

7. Cover with remaining potato, smoothing the top with a broad knife dipped in milk.

8. Score into squares and mark the edge with a fork.

9. Put pie into a moderate oven, 180–190°C, to reheat until a pale brown colour.

10. Serve garnished with parsley.

Serves 2

CROQUETTES

INGREDIENTS

1 quantity panada (see p. 224)
250 g cooked meat, chopped or minced
2 teaspoons chopped parsley
1 tablespoon chopped cooked
onion or shallot
¼ teaspoon salt
⅛ teaspoon pepper
dry breadcrumbs
1 egg, beaten

METHOD

1. Make the panada.

2. Add chopped or minced meat, parsley, onion and seasoning.

3. Turn onto plate; spread evenly and leave to cool.

4. When cold cut into six or eight lengths and shape like corks using two spatulas or large knives.

5. Coat with very fine, dry crumbs then with beaten egg and once more with crumbs.

6. Fry 5 minutes in heated oil, drain well on paper towel.

7. Serve on hot plate garnished with parsley.

Note: Substitutes for cooked meat: cooked chicken, turkey, or ham, cooked chopped vegetable mixture, cooked flaked fish or tinned fish.

Serves 3–4

TO REHEAT COLD ROAST BEEF OR LAMB

METHOD

1. Cut meat into slices.

2. Bring gravy to boiling point.

3. Reduce the heat and place the slices in, simmer just long enough to heat right through.

SAVOURY DISHES

These can be made from a wide variety of foods and provide suitable dishes for luncheons, teas and suppers. In this section dishes with the following MAIN ingredients are provided:

Legumes Nuts Cheese Eggs Cereals

VEGETABLE AU GRATIN

INGREDIENTS

2 cups any single vegetable or mixture of cooked vegetables
1 cup basic white masking sauce (see p. 224)
½ cup grated cheese
1 tablespoon dried breadcrumbs
1 tablespoon butter

METHOD

1. Place vegetable in an ovenproof dish.

2. Mask with masking sauce (see p. 224).

3. Sprinkle with grated cheese and breadcrumbs.

4. Dot butter in small pieces on top.

5. Bake in a moderately hot oven, 180–200°C, until a golden brown—10 to 15 minutes.

Serves 4

BEAN AND ONION CASSEROLE

INGREDIENTS

1 small onion, peeled and sliced
1 tablespoon margarine
Salt and pepper to taste
½ teaspoon curry powder
¼ cup stock or water
1 small apple, diced
1 grated carrot
1 large tomato, sliced
½ cup cooked soya or haricot beans
1 tablespoon grated cheese
1 tablespoon breadcrumbs

METHOD

1. Fry onion in margarine.

2. Add salt, pepper and curry. Cook 1 minute.

3. Add stock.

4. Add apple, carrot, tomato and cooked beans.

5. Cook gently for 10 minutes, stirring all the time.

6. Place in greased casserole dish.

7. Sprinkle with cheese and breadcrumbs.

8. Brown in 180°C oven for 15 to 20 minutes.

VARIATION
Omit cheese, sprinkle with breadcrumbs, heat in oven, 180°C, in covered casserole for 15 to 20 minutes. Serve with bacon rolls (p. 30).

Serves 2

STUFFED VEGETABLES

INGREDIENTS

Vegetables: use tomatoes (4), capsicum (4), marrow or squash
1 cup finely chopped cold meat, fish or chicken or 2 finely chopped hard-cooked eggs or 3 tablespoons grated cheese or 1 cup whole corn, beans or cold cooked brown rice
1 tablespoon chopped parsley
A little grated nutmeg
Pinch pepper
1 teaspoon salt
1 tablespoon butter or margarine

METHOD

1. Wash and dry vegetable.

2. Cut a slice from the stalk end of the vegetable and remove seeds from capsicum, marrow and squash.

3. Scoop out inside of vegetable, mash and mix approximately 2 tablespoons of this with all the ingredients.

4. Place mixture in vegetable shell.

5. Sprinkle with breadcrumbs.

6. Place small piece of butter or margarine on each.

7. Replace vegetable top.

8. Bake in a moderate oven, 180–190°C, for 15 to 20 minutes or until tender.

9. Serve on slices of toast and garnish with small sprigs of parsley.

Serves 4

CHEESE BALLS

INGREDIENTS

¼ cup plain or wholemeal flour
Pinch salt and cayenne
½ cup grated cheese
1 egg
Squeeze lemon juice
Oil

METHOD

1. Sift flour, salt and cayenne.

2. Mix cheese with flour.

3. Separate yolk from white of egg.

4. Beat yolk and lemon juice together and mix with dry ingredients.

5. Add stiffly beaten egg white.

6. Heat oil in frying pan.

7. Drop in small portions of mixture.

8. Fry until a light brown.

9. Drain on absorbent paper.

10. Serve hot, sprinkled with grated cheese.

Makes 12

BAKED CHEESE CUSTARD

INGREDIENTS

3 eggs
½ cup soft white breadcrumbs
1 cup milk
¼ teaspoon salt
½ teaspoon mustard
½ cup grated cheese

METHOD

1. Beat egg whites until stiff.

2. To the slightly beaten egg yolks add breadcrumbs, milk, salt, mustard and cheese.

3. Fold in egg whites.

4. Turn into a buttered, uncovered ovenproof dish.

5. Bake in a slow oven, 150–180°C, for 30 to 40 minutes or until a knife inserted in the centre comes out clean.

6. Serve hot, or cold with salad.

Serves 4

CHEESE SOUFFLÉ

INGREDIENTS

3 tablespoons butter or margarine
3 tablespoons plain flour
¼ teaspoon salt
Pinch cayenne pepper
1 cup milk
1 cup grated dry cheese
3 eggs

METHOD

1. Melt butter in saucepan.

2. Add flour, salt and cayenne; stir well.

3. Add milk and stir over slow heat until thick.

4. Add cheese and stir until just melted.

5. Separate whites from yolks of eggs.

6. Stir the sauce mixture into the yolks and allow to cool.

7. Beat egg whites in a bowl until stiff.

8. Fold gently into the cheese mixture.

9. Place into a well-greased oven-proof dish with

mixture at least 2 cm from the top of the dish.

10. Bake in a slow oven, 150–180°C, for 30 to 40 minutes.

11. Serve at once on heated plates.

Serves 4

QUICK QUICHE

INGREDIENTS

3 eggs
1½ cups milk
4 chopped bacon rashers
½ cup grated tasty cheese
1 grated onion
3 chopped shallots
2 tablespoons chopped parsley
2 tablespoons finely chopped red capsicum (optional)
350 g packet pastry mix

METHOD

1. Preheat oven to 200°C.

2. Grease two pie plates.

3. Beat eggs, add milk, bacon, cheese, onion, shallots, parsley and pastry mix. Mix well.

4. Pour into pie plates.

5. Bake 30 minutes.

Serves 8

CORN FRITTERS

INGREDIENTS

1 small can sweet corn (whole kernel)
1 quantity fritter batter (see p. 145)
Oil

METHOD

1. Half fill a deep saucepan with oil.

2. Pour the liquid off and put corn into batter. Mix well.

3. Put a spoonful of the mixture into the hot oil and fry until a golden brown.

4. Lift out with a slice or iron spoon and drain on absorbent paper.

5. Serve on a hot dish or plate, and garnish with sprigs of parsley.

Makes 12

CHEESE AND VEGETABLE BAKE

INGREDIENTS

3 large ripe tomatoes
2 large white onions
2 or 3 bacon rashers
1 cup fresh breadcrumbs
2 cups grated cheese
Pepper and salt to taste
1 teaspoon dry mustard
2 cups mashed potatoes
Milk for glazing

METHOD

1. Peel tomatoes and slice thickly.

2. Peel onions and slice thinly.

3. Remove rind and chop bacon finely.

4. Grease an ovenproof dish.

5. Fill with alternate layers of tomatoes, breadcrumbs, onion, cheese and bacon.

6. Sprinkle each layer with salt, pepper and mustard.

7. Spread mashed potato on top.

8. Glaze with milk.

9. Bake in a moderate oven, 180–200°C, for about 40 minutes.

Serves 4–6

CHEESE AND VEGETABLE PIE

INGREDIENTS

1 stick celery
1 small onion
½ turnip
1 small carrot
½ cup shelled peas
1 ¼ cups of Melted Butter Sauce 3 (see p. 224)
Double quantity shortcrust pastry (see p. 150)
½ cup grated cheese
Milk for glazing

METHOD

1. Prepare vegetables and cut into dice.

2. Cook vegetables until tender (any leftover cold vegetables could be used).

3. Combine vegetables with sauce.

4. Cut pastry in halves.

5. Roll one portion and line a lightly greased 20 cm pie plate.

6. Fill with vegetable mixture.

7. Sprinkle with cheese.

8. Roll out the remaining pastry and cover the mixture, pressing edges firmly.

9. Glaze with milk.

10. Bake in a hot oven, 220–230°C, for about 20 minutes.

Note: Mashed potato may be used instead of pastry to make this dish.

Serves 4–6

EGG AND BACON PIE

INGREDIENTS

Double quantity shortcrust pastry (see p. 150)
3–4 rashers bacon
6 eggs
¼ teaspoon salt
Pepper to taste
1 tablespoon chopped parsley

METHOD

1. Line a lightly greased 20 cm pie plate with half the pastry.

2. Remove rind and chop bacon; sprinkle half in the pie plate.

3. Break whole egg and place on bacon in pie plate, add seasoning and parsley.

4. Sprinkle with remainder of chopped bacon.

5. Glaze edge of pastry and roll remaining pastry to fit top.

6. Press the edges together and cut a slit in the middle of the pie.

7. Glaze the pastry and decorate.

8. Bake at 230°C for 10 minutes; reduce heat to 180°C and cook a further 20 to 25 minutes.

Serves 4

CURRIED EGGS

INGREDIENTS

½ cup rice
3 tablespoons butter
2 teaspoons curry powder
3 tablespoons plain flour
¼ teaspoon salt
1¼ cups milk
Squeeze lemon juice
4 hard-cooked eggs

METHOD

1. Boil rice according to recipe on page 8.

2. Heat butter in saucepan.

3. Add curry powder, flour and salt, and stir 1 minute.

4. Add milk, stir until boiling, and cook for 3 minutes; add lemon juice.

5. Shell the eggs, cut lengthwise into quarters, put into curry sauce and stand at side of heat for 15 minutes; it must not boil.

6. Serve on a hot dish or plate with a border of boiled rice, and garnish with slices of lemon and finely chopped parsley.

Serves 2

MORNAY

INGREDIENTS

125 g salmon or tuna or scallops or oysters or cooked fish or chicken or 6 hard-cooked eggs cut into wedges
½ teaspoon lemon juice
Salt and cayenne to taste
1¼ cups basic white masking sauce (see p. 224)
1 tablespoon grated cheese
1 tablespoon dried breadcrumbs

METHOD

1. Add lemon juice, salt, cayenne and one main ingredient to sauce.

2. Grease an ovenproof dish.

3. Place mixture into greased dish.

4. Sprinkle cheese and breadcrumbs on top.

5. Brown lightly in oven or under griller.

6. Serve garnished with parsley or lemon wedges.

Serves 2

LENTIL AND EGG CURRY

INGREDIENTS

1 cup dried red lentils
2 medium-size onions
3 tablespoons butter
1 tablespoon curry powder
¼ cup water
4 hard-cooked eggs
½ teaspoon salt

METHOD

1. Peel and slice onions.

2. Melt butter in saucepan. Add onions and curry powder.

3. Cook slowly for 10 minutes, stirring frequently.

4. Add water and lentils.

5. Cover and cook gently over low heat for 45 minutes or until lentils are tender.

6. Slice eggs and add with salt to the lentil mixture.

7. Mix gently and cook slowly for 5 minutes.

8. Serve hot.

Serves 4

MINCE AND CHEESE BURGERS

INGREDIENTS

1 kg (3½ cups) minced steak
½ teaspoon salt
Pinch pepper
2 finely grated onions
1 cup fresh breadcrumbs
Bread rolls
Cheese slices
Tomato slices

METHOD

1. Mould the meat, salt, pepper, onion and breadcrumbs well together into 12 or more thin shapes to fit bread roll.

2. Fry or grill the mixture for 5 to 10 minutes.

3. Place on bread roll with cheese and tomato slices.

4. Serve with salad.

Makes 12

MACARONI CHEESE

INGREDIENTS

60 g macaroni
2 tablespoons butter
2 tablespoons plain flour
1 ¼ cups milk
1 teaspoon mustard
½ teaspoon salt
Pinch cayenne pepper
½ cup grated cheese

METHOD

1. Have ready a saucepan of boiling salted water.

2. Break macaroni into 2 cm pieces and wash well.

3. Drop macaroni into boiling water; boil for 12 to 15 minutes, or until tender, with lid off the saucepan.

4. Drain.

5. Melt butter in saucepan.

6. Add flour off the heat; mix thoroughly, and cook gently for 1 minute (it must not be allowed to brown).

7. Add milk; stir until boiling.

8. Season with mustard, salt and cayenne pepper.

9. Add macaroni and half the cheese to sauce.

10. Pour into a greased pie dish.

11. Sprinkle remainder of cheese on top; dot a few pieces of butter round the edge of dish.

12. Brown in a hot oven or under a hot griller.

Note: Any variety of pasta may be used instead of macaroni.

Serves 2

POTATO PUFFS

INGREDIENTS

6 medium-sized old potatoes
2 teaspoons butter
1 tablespoon milk
1 egg
Salt and pepper to taste

METHOD

1. Wash, dry and bake potatoes in jackets.

2. Cut potatoes in halves.

3. Remove inside of potato,

being careful not to break skin.

4. Mash the removed potato, adding butter, milk, egg yolk, salt and pepper.

5. Stiffly beat white of egg and mix in lightly.

6. Fill potato cases.

7. Stand in a baking dish and place in a hot oven, 220–250°C, for 10 minutes to brown.

8. Serve on a hot dish or plate, garnished with sprigs of parsley.

Note: Finely chopped cold meat or grated cheese may be added to the mixture.

Serves 6

NUT ROAST

INGREDIENTS

1 small onion
4 medium tomatoes
¾ cup finely chopped mixed nuts
2 tablespoons oil
½ teaspoon salt
Pinch pepper
Chopped parsley
1 teaspoon vegetable extract
5 tablespoons water
1 egg, beaten
2 cups cooked mashed potatoes
2 tablespoons melted shortening

METHOD

1. Peel and dice onion and tomatoes.

2. Fry onion and nuts in oil until lightly brown.

3. Combine with all other ingredients except shortening.

4. Press into prepared tin and brush with oil.

5. Cover with foil.

6. Bake at 160–190°C for about 1 hour. Baste with melted shortening during cooking.

7. Serve with heated brown gravy (see p. 225).

Serves 4

FRIED RICE

INGREDIENTS

3 tablespoons butter
1 cup rice
1 cup finely diced celery
3 stock cubes or chicken noodle soup to make 3 cups of stock
Salt and pepper to taste
1 cup diced onion or shallots
1 cup finely diced capsicum
250 g bacon or ham
3 eggs

METHOD

1. Heat butter in heavy pan and add dry rice and celery.

2. Cook quickly stirring all the time, until a golden brown colour.

3. Add stock and salt and pepper. Bring to boil and simmer, with pan covered, until stock has been absorbed; stir occasionally.

4. Prepare onion and capsicum; remove rind and cut bacon into dice.

5. In another pan fry bacon, then onions in the bacon fat. Stir in capsicum and heat through.

6. Lightly beat eggs, fry until set and cut into small strips.

7. When rice is cooked fold in all other ingredients. Allow to reheat and serve.

Serves 4

SAVOURY DIPS

CHEESE DIP

INGREDIENTS

125 g cream cheese
½ cup cream
1 tablespoon tomato sauce
1 tablespoon chutney
1 tablespoon Worcestershire sauce
1 tablespoon finely chopped onion
1 tablespoon finely chopped capsicum
1 cup grated tasty cheese

METHOD

1. Add all ingredients except grated cheese to basin. Mix well.

2. Fold in grated cheese.

Asparagus and Ham Dip

INGREDIENTS

1 small can asparagus cuts
60 g ham
1 hard-cooked egg
½ cup melted butter masking
sauce (see p. 224)
Salt and pepper to taste

METHOD

1. Drain asparagus.

2. Finely dice ham and chop egg.

3. Add these ingredients to masking sauce. Mix evenly, adding salt and pepper to taste.

Note: This can also be served on hot, buttered toast.

Basic Risotto

INGREDIENTS

60 g butter
1 onion
375 g long grain rice
3 cups chicken stock or 2
chicken stock cubes crumbled
in 3 cups hot water
Pinch of saffron
Salt and pepper to taste

METHOD

1. Heat butter in a heavy pan, add peeled and finely chopped onion and cook gently until the onion is golden brown.

2. Add rice and stir until grains are coated with the butter mixture.

3. Gradually add chicken stock stirring all the time until the stock has been absorbed by the rice. This should take from 25 to 30 minutes. Rice should be tender and separate.

4. Add saffron.

5. Serve on a hot plate garnished with parsley.

Serves 4–6

SPAGHETTI BOLOGNAISE

INGREDIENTS

500 g (1 ¾ cups) round steak, minced
2 cups tomato puree
3 tablespoons butter or oil
1 small onion, grated or chopped finely
3 thin slices of garlic
Salt and pepper to taste
½ teaspoon mixed herbs
1 teaspoon sugar
250 g spaghetti

METHOD

1. Place meat, tomato puree, butter, onion, garlic and seasonings in saucepan.

2. Bring to the boil and simmer gently 1 ½ hours.

3. Twenty minutes before serving, cook the spaghetti: place into 2 cups boiling salted water, boil gently until tender—about 12 minutes.

4. Spread the spaghetti on a large serving dish, cover with the meat mixture.

5. Sprinkle with parmesan cheese, and garnish with sprigs of parsley.

Serves 4

SAVOURY OMELETTE

INGREDIENTS

2 eggs
¼ teaspoon finely chopped parsley
¼ teaspoon each of thyme and marjoram, or any suitable savoury flavourings
Pinch salt
Pinch pepper
1 tablespoon butter

METHOD

1. Separate whites from yolks of eggs.

2. Beat yolks; add parsley, thyme, marjoram, salt and pepper.

3. Beat whites until very stiff.

4. Mix very lightly with the seasoned yolks.

5. Heat omelette pan slowly.

6. Melt butter in pan; pour in mixture; allow to set over a gentle heat.

7. Brown very slightly on top either by putting under hot griller or turning very carefully with a large knife.

8. Serve on a very hot dish at once.

Note: Use eggs at room temperature.

Serves 1

MUSHROOM GRATINEE

INGREDIENTS

2 eggs
Freshly ground nutmeg
¼ teaspoon salt
Freshly ground black pepper
1¾ cups milk, boiling
1 cup grated cheese
500 g old potatoes, peeled and thinly sliced
250 g flat mushrooms, wiped, trimmed and sliced
½ cup soft white breadcrumbs
2 tablespoons melted butter or margarine

METHOD

1. Beat eggs with nutmeg, salt and pepper.

2. Stir in the boiling milk and half the cheese.

3. Arrange potatoes and mushrooms in layers in a greased baking dish, pouring a little of the milk mixture over each layer.

4. Sprinkle with remaining cheese and breadcrumbs.

5. Spoon over melted butter.

6. Bake in a moderate oven, 180°C, for 50 to 60 minutes or until the potatoes are tender.

7. Serve hot accompanied by a salad.

Serves 4

TOMATO AND VEGETABLE SAVOURY

INGREDIENTS

1 cup diced celery
1 cup diced carrot
½ cup peas
750 g cooked minced steak
2 tomatoes
1 cup cooked rice
1 can (500 g) tomato soup
½ cup grated cheese
1 small packet potato chips or
½ cup dried breadcrumbs

METHOD

1. Cook celery, carrots and peas until tender.

2. Grease ovenproof dish.

3. Place half mince in dish, and cover with half the vegetables.

4. Cover with sliced tomato and half the rice.

5. Pour over half the tomato soup.

6. Repeat layers.

7. Sprinkle with grated cheese and chips or breadcrumbs.

8. Bake at 180–200°C until heated right through and browned on top—30 to 40 minutes.

Serves 6

WELSH RAREBIT

INGREDIENTS

125 g cheese
1 tablespoon butter
1 teaspoon mustard
Cayenne pepper
2 tablespoons milk or cream
2 teaspoons Worcestershire sauce
4 slices buttered toast

METHOD

1. Slice cheese thinly or grate and mix together with butter, mustard, cayenne, milk and sauce.

2. Spread on toast.

3. Place under griller or in top of oven for 3 to 4 minutes.

4. Serve very hot.

Serves 2 or 4

POTATO FRITTERS

INGREDIENTS

4 large potatoes
2 eggs
1 small onion
Salt and pepper to taste
2 tablespoons flour
Fat or oil

METHOD

1. Wash and peel potatoes.

2. Remove skin from onion.

3. Grate potatoes and onion coarsely into a sieve or colander. Press moisture from the mixture.

4. Place mixture into a basin, add flour, salt and pepper.

5. Beat eggs and add to mixture.

6. Heat fat or oil until a blue haze or fume rises from the surface.

7. Place spoonfuls of the mixture into the fat and fry until golden brown on both sides.

8. Drain on kitchen paper.

9. Serve on a hot plate garnished with parsley.

SWEETCORN BAKE

INGREDIENTS

15 g margarine
2 teaspoons flour
⅓ cup evaporated milk
¼ teaspoon salt
Pinch pepper
150 g asparagus cuts
65 g creamed sweet corn
1 hard-cooked egg
¼ cup grated tasty cheese
1 tablespoon breadcrumbs

METHOD

1. Melt margarine and add flour. Cook for 1 minute.

2. Remove from heat and add milk slowly.

3. Return to heat and stir until thick.

4. Add salt, pepper, asparagus and corn.

5. Place half of mixture into casserole dish—top with sliced egg and remaining mixture.

6. Sprinkle with cheese and breadcrumbs.

7. Bake in a moderate oven until golden.

Serves 2

LENTIL STEW

INGREDIENTS

1 cup red lentils
4 cups meat stock or 4 cups
water and 4 beef cubes
1 large onion
1 large stick celery
1 carrot
1 parsnip
1 small swede turnip
1 small capsicum
125 g mushrooms
2 tablespoons margarine or
butter
2 sliced cloves garlic
1 tablespoon plain flour
½ teaspoon dried mixed herbs
Pepper and salt as desired

METHOD

1. Wash and drain lentils, leave soaking in stock or water.

2. Wash, peel and finely dice all the hard vegetables.

3. Wash, seed and chop capsicum.

4. Wash and chop mushrooms.

5. Heat margarine or butter in a large saucepan, add onion, cook and stir until browned but not burned. Add garlic and mushrooms, cook 5 minutes.

6. Stir in flour, cook 1 minute.

7. Stir in other diced vegetables, followed by lentils and liquid.

8. Stir until boiling, add herbs and seasoning.

9. Reduce heat, cover and simmer slowly for 45 minutes.

10. Serve garnished with chopped parsley and with mashed potato, boiled beans or peas for a main meal or on toast for lunch.

VARIATION: LENTIL LOAF

1. Grate hard vegetables, chop others finely.

2. Reduce liquid to 2 cups.

3. Simmer 15 minutes then transfer mixture to a well-greased 22 cm × 11 cm × 6.5 cm loaf tin. Press down. Cover with a mixture of 3 tablespoons breadcrumbs, 2 tablespoons grated cheese and 1 tablespoon desiccated coconut.

4. Bake in a moderate oven for 45 minutes.

5. Turn onto heated plate, crumbed top up.

6. Serve hot with cauliflower or broccoli in white sauce and jacket potatoes or cold with salad.

Serves 6

BEEF
AND VEGETABLES
WITH NOODLES

INGREDIENTS

150 g blade steak
5 shallots
1 stick celery
½ large carrot
⅓ green capsicum
1 tablespoon oil
1 beef stock cube
1 tablespoon cornflour
½ cup cold water
1 tablespoon soy sauce
50 g noodles
¼ can mushrooms

METHOD

1. Slice steak into strips.

2. Prepare vegetables; slice shallots, cut celery in diagonal slices, peel carrot and cut into thin strips and cut capsicum into thin strips.

3. Heat oil in frypan and brown meat, remove and drain on kitchen paper.

4. Add celery, capsicum and carrot to hot oil and cook a few minutes.

5. In a small bowl, crumble stock cube, add cornflour and a little of the water to blend. Add the rest of the water and the soy sauce.

6. Half fill a large saucepan with hot water, place on the stove and bring to the boil. When water is boiling, add the noodles and cook with lid off until tender (5 to 8 minutes).

7. Return meat to frypan, add mushrooms and shallots, stir, and heat through.

8. Add stock to frypan stirring all the time. Simmer until sauce thickens.

9. Serve with cooked noodles.

Serves 2

SAVOURY DISHES

LASAGNE

INGREDIENTS

1 tablespoon oil or margarine
250 g minced beef
1 chopped onion
1 clove garlic, crushed
½ cup canned or cooked
tomatoes
1 tablespoon tomato paste
½ teaspoon salt
Pepper to taste
¼ teaspoon dried mixed herbs
125 g lasagne pasta
4 slices mozzarella cheese
60 g cottage or ricotta cheese

METHOD

1. Heat oil in saucepan, add
beef, onion and garlic; cook
until brown.

2. Add tomatoes, tomato
paste, salt, pepper and
herbs; simmer 30 minutes.

3. Boil a large saucepan of
water, add lasagne pasta and
cook for 20 minutes. Drain.

4. Arrange alternate layers
of pasta, meat sauce,
mozzarella and ricotta
cheese in a greased
casserole.

5. Bake in a moderate
oven, 190°C, for 30
minutes.

Serves 4

TUNA AND
PUMPKIN RISSOLES

INGREDIENTS

2 medium potatoes
150 g pumpkin
1 185 g can tuna
1 tablespoon chopped parsley
1 small onion, diced
1 chicken stock cube
½ teaspoon curry powder
¾ cup dried breadcrumbs
1–2 tablespoons
polyunsaturated oil

METHOD

1. Peel potatoes and
pumpkin. Cut into large
pieces. Boil until soft.

2. Drain and mash.

3. Add tuna, parsley, onion,
stock cube and curry
powder. Mix well.

4. Divide mixture into 12 portions. Shape into rounds.

5. Roll in breadcrumbs.

6. Heat oil in pan, fry rissoles. Cook until brown on each side.

7. Serve hot with vegetables, or cold with salad.

Makes 12

CRUSTY MINCE AND SPINACH ROLLS

INGREDIENTS

6 crusty wholemeal bread rolls
1 teaspoon oil
5 green shallots, chopped
250 g minced steak
8 spinach leaves, chopped (green part only)
¾ cup water
2 tablespoons tomato paste
1 teaspoon Worcestershire sauce
1 teaspoon grated lemon rind
½ teaspoon nutmeg
1 tablespoon cornflour
1 tablespoon water (extra)

250 g carton low-fat cottage cheese
2 tablespoons chopped parsley

METHOD

1. Cut tops off bread rolls.

2. Hollow out centre of each roll and make into breadcrumbs.

3. Heat oil in pan, add shallots, mince and spinach. Cook, stirring, until mince is browned.

4. Add water, tomato paste, Worcestershire sauce, lemon rind and nutmeg; bring to boil and reduce heat. Simmer for 2 minutes.

5. Stir in blended cornflour and extra water, stir until mixture boils and thickens.

6. Remove from heat, stir in breadcrumbs, cheese and parsley.

7. Spoon mixture into bread rolls, replace tops, wrap each roll in foil.

8. Bake on oven trays in moderate oven for 15 minutes or until heated through.

Makes 6

SPINACH PIE

INGREDIENTS

20 sheets filo pastry
110 g margarine or butter,
melted
1 bunch spinach (green part
only)
½ teaspoon grated nutmeg or
½ whole nutmeg grated
100 g grated cheese
150 g fetta, ricotta or cottage
cheese
6 eggs

METHOD

1. Cut filo pastry to size of tin.

2. Grease lamington tin.

3. Place about 10 sheets of filo pastry in the tin, brushing melted butter or margarine lightly between each sheet.

4. In a bowl, combine shredded spinach, nutmeg, cheeses and beaten eggs, mix well.

5. Place this mixture on top of filo pastry in lamington tin, then layer remaining filo on top, brushing between each sheet with melted butter or margarine.

6. Place in oven for approximately 20 to 30 minutes at 190°C.

Serves 6–8

ZUCCHINI SLICE

INGREDIENTS

400 g zucchini
1 large onion
4 rashers of bacon
¾ cup grated cheddar cheese
1 cup self-raising flour
½ cup oil or melted butter or
margarine
5 eggs
Salt and pepper to taste

METHOD

1. Coarsely grate unpeeled zucchini.

2. Chop onion and bacon finely.

3. Combine zucchini, onion, bacon, cheese, sifted flour, oil and lightly beaten eggs.

4. Season with salt and pepper.

5. Pour into well-greased lamington pan (base measures 16 cm × 26 cm).

6. Bake in moderate oven for 30 to 40 minutes or until browned.

Note: If preferred, 400 g of carrot may be substituted for the zucchini in this recipe.

Serves 4–6

VEGETABLE STRUDEL

INGREDIENTS

1 tablespoon oil
1 stick celery, sliced
2 grated carrots
¼ chopped capsicum, seeds removed
¼ cup frozen peas
Chives
100 g cottage cheese
Salt and pepper to taste
10 sheets filo pastry
50 g butter or margarine
1 tablespoon sesame seeds

METHOD

1. Preheat oven to 200°C.

2. Lightly grease oven tray or lamington tin.

3. Heat oil in frypan—add celery, carrot and capsicum and fry over moderate heat until vegetables have softened slightly.

4. Add peas and chives and cook for one minute longer.

5. Remove from heat, cool slightly, add cottage cheese and mix well; season with salt and pepper.

6. To assemble, lay one sheet of filo pastry on bench, and brush lightly with melted butter or margarine. Place another sheet of pastry on top and brush again with melted butter or margarine. Continue until all sheets of pastry are used. Spoon vegetable mixture down central column of pastry, then fold one side over vegetables, then the other. Turn strudel under at each end, then turn the whole strudel over. Brush over with melted butter or margarine and sprinkle with sesame seeds.

7. Bake in oven for 25 to 30 minutes.

Serves 4–6

MOUSSAKA

INGREDIENTS

1 thickly sliced eggplant
Salt
1 tablespoon oil
1 chopped onion
1 clove garlic, crushed
500 g minced lamb or beef
1 400 g can tomatoes
½ teaspoon oregano
Pepper to taste
½ cup cottage or ricotta cheese
2 eggs
¼ teaspoon nutmeg

METHOD

1. Place eggplant in a colander and sprinkle with salt. Cover and stand for 30 minutes.

2. Heat oil in a saucepan and saute onion and garlic until soft and golden.

3. Add meat and cook until brown.

4. Add tomatoes, oregano and pepper and simmer for 10 minutes.

5. Drain eggplant, pat dry with a paper towel.

6. Brush eggplant slices with oil and grill for 5 minutes each side. (Eggplant slices may be fried if preferred.)

7. Layer eggplant and meat sauce in a greased casserole dish.

8. Lightly beat cottage cheese and eggs and pour over mixture in casserole.

9. Sprinkle with nutmeg and bake in a moderate oven, 190°C, for 40 minutes until top is golden brown.

Serves 6

CANNELLONI

FILLING

INGREDIENTS

500 g minced steak
½ cup breadcrumbs
2 tablespoons water
1 medium onion, chopped
2 tablespoons ricotta cheese or
¼ cup cream
1 egg

1 tablespoon chopped parsley
½ teaspoon oregano
½ teaspoon basil
1 teaspoon salt
¼ teaspoon pepper
1 clove garlic, crushed
16 tubes cannelloni

METHOD

1. Place minced steak, breadcrumbs, onion, water, ricotta cheese, beaten egg, parsley, oregano, basil, salt, pepper and garlic into a basin and mix well.

2. Fill cannelloni with meat mixture.

3. Place in a single layer in a greased casserole dish.

SAUCE

INGREDIENTS

1 tablespoon oil
1 chopped onion
½ teaspoon oregano
½ teaspoon basil
1 clove garlic, crushed
250 g tomato paste
2 cups water
¼ teaspoon pepper
½ cup grated parmesan cheese

METHOD

1. Heat oil in a saucepan, add onion and cook until soft.

2. Add oregano, basil, garlic, tomato paste, water and pepper.

3. Simmer gently for 5 minutes.

4. Pour sauce over cannelloni in casserole dish.

5. Sprinkle parmesan cheese over cannelloni and sauce.

6. Bake in a moderate oven, 180°C, for 40 minutes.

7. Serve with a tossed green salad (see p. 70).

Serves 6–8

CHEESE FONDUE

INGREDIENTS

2 cups grated Emmenthaler cheese
2 cups grated gruyere cheese
1 tablespoon flour
Pinch cayenne pepper
1 cup apple juice
1 cup grape juice (white)

METHOD

1. Combine grated cheeses, flour and pepper.

2. Heat juices in heavy saucepan or fondue pan.

3. When boiling add 1 tablespoon of cheese, stir until melted. Reduce heat to simmer.

4. Continue to add cheese tablespoonful at a time until all is melted.

5. Keep hot while dipping cubes of bread.

Serves 4

STIR-FRIED BEEF AND VEGETABLES

INGREDIENTS

1–3 tablespoons vegetable oil
4 cups assorted cut vegetables (choose from red and green capsicum strips, julienne carrots, onion wedges, broccoli florets, sliced fresh mushrooms and canned water chestnuts)
1 clove garlic, sliced
Few slices fresh peeled ginger

500 g lean boneless beef, cut into very thin strips
1 cup cold water
2 teaspoons cornflour
1 beef stock cube, crushed
2 tablespoons soy sauce
1 tablespoon stir-fry sauce

METHOD

1. Heat half the oil in a frying pan until hot.

2. Add vegetables, garlic and ginger.

3. Stir-fry for 5 minutes and remove from heat.

4. Heat remaining oil until a blue haze rises, add beef and stir-fry until browned.

5. Blend together the remaining ingredients.

6. Add to the beef with the vegetable mixture.

7. Cook and stir until thickened and clear.

8. Serve over hot, cooked, brown rice.

Serves 4

MILK PUDDINGS

BREAD AND BUTTER CUSTARD

INGREDIENTS

1 tablespoon sultanas
1 thin slice buttered bread
1 egg
1 tablespoon sugar
1¼ cups milk
3 drops vanilla essence
Nutmeg

METHOD

1. Place prepared sultanas in a greased ovenproof dish.

2. Cut the buttered bread into small squares or finger lengths.

3. Place in dish.

4. Beat egg and sugar together, add milk and essence, and beat well.

5. Pour over bread.

6. Grate nutmeg over top, and wipe edges of dish.

7. Stand in a baking dish half full of cold water and place in a slow oven, 150–160°C, and cook until set, from 20 to 30 minutes (when cooked, a knife-blade inserted in the centre will be free from mixture).

8. Remove immediately from hot water.

Note: This custard may be steamed. Follow method as above but cover dish with greased paper and cook in a steamer. Test as above and remove immediately from hot water.

Serves 2

ANGEL'S FOOD

INGREDIENTS

1 egg (60 g)
1 cup milk
2 tablespoons sugar
3 teaspoons gelatine
2 tablespoons hot water
5 drops vanilla essence

METHOD

1. Separate white from yolk of egg.

2. Heat milk and sugar, pour onto egg yolk, and mix well.

3. Return to saucepan, heat gently, stirring well without boiling, until mixture coats the spoon.

4. Cool.

5. Dissolve gelatine in hot water. Add to cool custard mixture with vanilla.

6. Beat egg white until stiff and fold lightly into mixture.

7. Pour into wet mould and set in refrigerator.

8. Turn out onto a serving dish.

Serves 2

BLANCMANGE

INGREDIENTS

2 tablespoons maize cornflour
1¼ cups milk
1 tablespoon sugar
Lemon rind or bay leaf or peach leaf
3 drops essence (optional)

METHOD

1. Rinse a mould or small basin with cold water.

2. Blend the cornflour with some of the milk.

3. Put the remainder of the milk on to boil in a small saucepan with sugar and bay leaf or lemon rind or peach leaf.

4. When nearly boiling, remove from stove, lift out leaf or rind and stir in the blended cornflour.

5. Stir well, return to stove, and cook for 3 minutes after it comes to the boil.

6. Add essence if required.

7. Pour into the wet mould.

8. Stand mould in a shallow basin of cold water to set. Chill.

9. When quite cold, loosen round edge, and turn it out into a serving dish.

10. Serve with jam, stewed fruit or custard.

Serves 4

RICE, MACARONI OR VERMICELLI CUSTARD

INGREDIENTS

1¼ cups water
Pinch salt
1 tablespoon rice, macaroni or vermicelli
1 egg
1 tablespoon sugar
1¼ cups milk
3 drops vanilla essence
1 teaspoon butter
Nutmeg

METHOD

1. Have a moderate oven ready.

2. Put water and salt on to boil.

3. When boiling add cereal.

4. Cook until soft, from 15 to 20 minutes.

5. Beat egg and sugar together, then add milk and vanilla.

6. When cereal is cooked, strain and mix with the custard mixture.

7. Pour into an ovenproof dish, sprinkle with nutmeg, and put small pieces of butter on top.

8. Wipe edges of dish.

9. Stand in a baking dish half full of cold water, place in a slow oven, 150–160°C, and bake until set, about 20 to 30 minutes (when cooked, a knife-blade inserted in the centre will be free from mixture).

10. Remove immediately from hot water.

Serves 2

SAGO CUSTARD

INGREDIENTS

1 tablespoon sago
⅔ cup water
Pinch salt
1 cup milk
1 tablespoon sugar
1 egg
3 drops vanilla essence
Nutmeg
1 teaspoon butter

METHOD

1. Have a moderate oven in readiness.

2. Wash sago.

3. Put water and salt on to boil.

4. Place the sago in the boiling water, and stir until it is quite transparent.

5. Add milk and sugar, and stir until well blended with the sago; remove from stove and cool.

6. Beat egg lightly, add with vanilla to the sago when cool.

7. Pour into an ovenproof dish, sprinkle with nutmeg, and place small pieces of butter on top.

8. Wipe edges of dish, and stand it in a baking dish half-full of cold water.

9. Bake in a slow oven, 150–160°C, until set—about 30 minutes (when cooked, a knife-blade inserted in the centre will be free from mixture).

10. Remove immediately from hot water.

Serves 2

SAGO OR TAPIOCA CREAM

INGREDIENTS

3 tablespoons sago or tapioca
½ cup cold water
2 cups milk
3 tablespoons sugar
2 eggs
Vanilla essence to taste

METHOD

1. Soak sago in the cold water for 10 minutes, soak tapioca overnight.

2. Place in a double saucepan with milk. Cook

sago for about 15 minutes, or until soft, stirring occasionally; tapioca 1 hour or until clear.

3. Mix sugar and egg yolks, add gradually, and stir a few minutes longer. Remove from stove.

4. Beat whites of eggs stiffly and pour the hot custard onto them gradually, stirring all the time.

5. Add vanilla.

6. When cool, place in serving dish.

Serves 4

SPANISH CREAM

Recipe as for Angel's Food (see p. 110), but add dissolved gelatine to the hot custard mixture; this allows a jelly to set at the base of the cream mixture.

Note: To add variety, flavour the milk before making the custard:

Add 1 teaspoon of cocoa for chocolate flavour.

Add 1 teaspoon of instant coffee for coffee flavour.

Add 1 tablespoon of caramel sauce and substitute brown sugar for white sugar for caramel flavour.

JUNKET

INGREDIENTS

½ junket tablet
1¼ cups fresh milk
1 teaspoon sugar
5 drops vanilla essence
Nutmeg

METHOD

1. Dissolve the tablet in 1 teaspoon water.

2. Warm milk to blood heat by placing it in a cup with sugar and vanilla, and standing cup in a basin of boiling water for 5 minutes.

3. Stir in the dissolved tablet.

4. Pour into a glass dish, grate nutmeg on top, and stand in a warm place to set.

5. Allow to cool.

Serves 2

STIRRED CUSTARD (1)

INGREDIENTS

1 cup milk
1 egg
1 tablespoon sugar
4 drops vanilla essence
Nutmeg

METHOD

1. Warm milk in a double saucepan or in a jug standing in saucepan of water.

2. Beat egg and sugar together until thick; add warm milk.

3. Return to double saucepan or jug.

4. Stir with a wooden spoon until the custard coats the spoon. Do not allow it to overheat or it will curdle.

5. Add vanilla. Cool.

6. Place in a serving dish or in custard glasses, with nutmeg grated on top.

Serves 2

STIRRED CUSTARD (2)

INGREDIENTS

1 teaspoon maize cornflour
1¼ cups milk
1 egg
1 tablespoon sugar
Vanilla essence to taste

METHOD

1. Blend cornflour with a little of the milk; put remainder of the milk on to boil in a saucepan.

2. When boiling, stir in cornflour, cook for 1 minute; allow to cool off stove.

3. When cool add egg and sugar beaten together; stand saucepan over boiling water and stir until custard coats the spoon (do not let it overheat); add vanilla.

Serves 2

BAKED RICE

INGREDIENTS

2 tablespoons rice
⅔ cup water
1¼ cups milk
1 tablespoon sugar
1 teaspoon butter
Nutmeg

METHOD

1. Wash rice if necessary.

2. Put rice in ovenproof dish, add water, and cook in slow oven until rice absorbs all the water.

3. Add milk, sugar, butter and grated nutmeg to rice; mix well.

4. Bake in a very slow oven from 1 to 1½ hours.

Note: Vanilla, lemon, cinnamon sticks are suitable flavourings. Rice may be boiled in a saucepan instead of being cooked in an ovenproof dish in the oven.

Serves 2

BRULEE

INGREDIENTS

3 whole eggs
1 egg yolk
30 g white sugar
1 cup cream
1 cup milk
vanilla flavouring
1 cup brown sugar

METHOD

1. Beat the eggs and white sugar until well blended.

2. Add milk and vanilla.

3. Pour into a 20 cm greased pie dish.

4. Stand the dish in a tray of cold water and bake in the middle of a moderate oven until set.

5. Remove from tray of water.

6. Cover the top of the custard evenly with sieved brown sugar.

7. Place under a moderate grill (not too close). Cook until sugar caramelises. Watch closely as sugar burns easily.

Serves 4

QUEEN PUDDING

INGREDIENTS

2 thin slices buttered bread or stale sponge cake
Jam
1 egg
2 tablespoons sugar
1 cup milk
Coloured sugar (see p. 247)

METHOD

1. Have a moderate oven in readiness.

2. Spread the buttered bread or sponge cake thinly with jam.

3. Cut in thin strips and place in an ovenproof dish until half filled.

4. Separate the white from the yolk of the egg.

5. Mix the yolk with 1 tablespoon sugar.

6. Warm the milk, but do not overheat.

7. Pour the warm milk onto the yolk and sugar, and mix well together.

8. Pour over bread or cake in dish.

9. Stand the ovenproof dish in a baking dish half-filled with cold water to prevent the custard from boiling while cooking.

10. Cook in a slow oven, 150–160°C, until set—about 30 minutes.

11. Allow to cool.

12. When cool, spread a thin layer of jam on top.

13. Beat the egg white to a stiff froth.

14. Add to it 1 tablespoon sugar. Beat until thick.

15. Pile lightly on top of the pudding.

16. Stand in a moderate oven until pale brown.

17. Sprinkle coloured sugar on top and serve.

Serves 2

SWEET POACHED EGGS

INGREDIENTS

*6 halves of preserved or
stewed apricots
1 quantity blancmange (see
p. 110)*

METHOD

1. Place each half apricot in
a cup or small mould,
keeping skin side
downwards.

2. Pour over sufficient
blancmange to cover the
apricot.

3. Set aside until cold, turn
out onto a serving dish.

Serves 3

BAKED CUSTARD

INGREDIENTS

*1 egg
1 tablespoon sugar
¾ cup milk
3 drops vanilla essence
Nutmeg*

METHOD

1. Have a moderate oven in
readiness.

2. Grease a small ovenproof
dish with a little butter.

3. Beat the egg with the
sugar until thick.

4. Add the milk and vanilla.

5. Pour mixture into the
buttered dish.

6. Grate nutmeg on top,
and wipe edges of dish.

7. Stand in a baking dish
half full of water; this
prevents the custard from
curdling while it is cooking.

8. Bake in a slow oven,
150–160°C, for 15 to 20
minutes or until set (when
cooked, a knife-blade
inserted in the centre will
be free from mixture).

9. Remove immediately
from hot water.

Note: This custard may be
steamed. Follow method as
above, but cover dish with
greased paper and cook in a
steamer. Test as above and
remove immediately from hot
water.

CARAMEL SPONGE

INGREDIENTS

80 g butter
1 cup brown sugar
2 cups milk
2 eggs, separated
1 tablespoon gelatine
¼ cup cold water

METHOD

1. Melt butter and brown sugar (do not boil) to make a caramel.

2. Boil milk and add gradually to butter and brown sugar. Stir until dissolved.

3. Beat egg yolks and add to milk mixture.

4. Pour into double saucepan and cook slowly over hot water until the mixture coats a spoon.

5. Allow to cool.

6. Add gelatine to cold water and stand in a container of hot water to dissolve gelatine.

7. Add dissolved gelatine to custard.

8. Beat egg whites until stiff and fold into the cold custard and gelatine mixture.

9. Pour into a wetted mould and allow to set.

Serves 4

ARROWROOT OR CORNFLOUR GRUEL

INGREDIENTS

1 tablespoon arrowroot or maize cornflour
1¼ cups milk
Pinch of salt
1 teaspoon of sugar
Nutmeg

METHOD

1. Blend arrowroot or cornflour with a little of the milk.

2. Put remainder of milk on to boil with salt and sugar.

3. When nearly boiling, remove from heat.

4. Add the blended

arrowroot or cornflour; stir
well.

5. Return to heat, bring to
the boil, and simmer for 3
minutes.

6. Stir well.

7. Serve in a small bowl or
cup.

8. Grate nutmeg on top.

9. Serve sippets of toast
separately on a small plate.

Serves 2

LIGHT BREAD
PUDDING

INGREDIENTS

*2 tablespoons fresh
breadcrumbs*
⅔ cup milk
1 tablespoon sugar
1 egg

METHOD

1. Grease a small pie dish.

2. Put breadcrumbs into a
basin.

3. Heat milk and pour onto
breadcrumbs.

4. Add sugar.

5. Separate white from yolk
of egg.

6. Stir yolk into milk and
breadcrumbs.

7. Beat white up stiffly, and
stir very lightly into
mixture.

8. Pour into greased pie
dish.

9. Stand pie dish in a
baking dish containing cold
water.

10. Bake in a slow oven,
150–160°C, for 10 to 15
minutes or until set.

11. Serve hot or cold.

Serves 2

MILK JELLY

INGREDIENTS

1½ teaspoons gelatine
2 tablespoons hot water
1 cup milk
3 teaspoons sugar
3 drops vanilla or other
suitable flavouring

METHOD

1. Dissolve gelatine in hot water.

2. Warm milk; add sugar and flavouring.

3. Stir in dissolved gelatine.

4. Pour into moulds or suitable dish.

5. Chill until set, and turn out.

Serves 2

STEAMED OR BOILED PUDDINGS

STEAMING

Two methods may be used:

1. Stand covered basin in steamer over a saucepan of gently boiling water.

2. Stand covered basin in saucepan with enough gently boiling water to reach halfway up the side of the basin. It will be necessary with this method to add extra boiling water while cooking—pour gently between the basin and the saucepan.

BOILING

Pudding cloth:

1. 45 cm square white sheeting.

2. Dip in boiling water, drain and squeeze water out.

3. Spread on plate, sprinkle well with flour before adding pudding mixture.

4. Gather edges evenly, tie firmly leaving 3 cm for expansion.

5. Place pudding into rapidly boiling water, add extra boiling water as required.

BASIN

Tie a floured pudding cloth firmly over the basin with string, tie opposite corners of cloth together on top. Place in a large saucepan containing enough boiling water to cover the pudding. Boil gently.

APPLE PUDDING

INGREDIENTS

3 apples
2 tablespoons sugar
3 cloves
1 quantity suet crust or
shortcrust pastry (see p. 150)
1 strip of lemon rind

METHOD

1. Peel, quarter, core and slice the apples.

2. Place on a plate with the sugar and cloves.

3. Put a saucepan of water on to boil.

4. Grease a small basin with butter and sprinkle with sugar.

5. Roll out two-thirds of the pastry into a round shape, and line the basin.

6. Put in the fruit, sugar, cloves and rind, piling high.

7. Wet round the edge of the pastry.

8. Roll out the remaining one-third of the pastry, and cover the basin, pressing the edges well together.

9. Pinch a frill around the edge.

10. For steaming cover with greaseproof paper or aluminium foil. For boiling tie a floured cloth firmly over the top of basin.

11. Cook for 1½ to 2 hours.

12. Turn onto a hot plate.

13. Serve with suitable sauce or custard.

Serves 4

QUICKLY MADE APPLE PUDDING

INGREDIENTS

6 cooking apples
2 cups water
4 tablespoons sugar
6 cloves
1 piece lemon rind
Double quantity suet crust or
shortcrust pastry (see p. 150)

METHOD

1. Peel, core and quarter apples.

2. Boil water, sugar, cloves

and lemon rind, add apples and cook gently with lid on.

3. Roll out the pastry to size of the saucepan lid. Make a hole in the centre.

4. Place in saucepan on top of boiling apples.

5. Cook gently with the lid on for 20 to 30 minutes.

6. Lift out pastry, cut into triangles and serve with apples on a hot plate.

Serves 6

SAGO PLUM PUDDING

INGREDIENTS

4 tablespoons sago
1 cup milk
¼ cup butter
½ cup sugar
1 teaspoon bicarbonate of soda
1 cup fresh breadcrumbs
¼ cup plain flour
¼ teaspoon salt
½ cup sultanas
½ cup raisins
½ cup chopped dates

METHOD

1. Soak sago in milk overnight.

2. Place saucepan of water on to boil over which the pudding is to steam.

3. Grease mould with butter and cut a piece of greaseproof paper or foil the same shape as the top of the mould, but 3 cm larger all round.

4. Beat butter and sugar.

5. Add sago, milk and soda.

6. Add breadcrumbs, sifted flour, salt and fruit and mix all lightly.

7. Place in prepared mould, cover with greaseproof paper or foil, and steam for 2½ to 3 hours.

8. Serve with suitable sauce or custard.

Serves 6

CHRISTMAS PUDDING

INGREDIENTS

500 g currants
500 g sultanas
250 g raisins
60 g citron peel
125 g almonds
500 g butter
500 g brown sugar
8 eggs
⅔ cup brandy
250 g soft breadcrumbs
250 g plain flour
Pinch salt
1 teaspoon bicarbonate of soda
½ teaspoon grated nutmeg
2 teaspoons mixed spice

METHOD

1. Clean and prepare all the fruit, cut the citron peel finely, blanch and chop the almonds.

2. Have a large boiler of water in readiness.

3. Cream the butter and sugar, add well-beaten eggs and brandy.

4. Stir all the fruit in well.

5. Add breadcrumbs, sifted flour, salt, soda, nutmeg and spice.

6. Mix all well together.

7. Tie up in a very strong pudding cloth, allowing room for it to swell.

8. Place in boiling water and cook for 6 hours. Cook a further 3 hours on the day it is to be eaten.

9. Serve with brandy or wine sauce, or stirred custard.

Note: This mixture may be steamed in one large or two medium basins. Allow 4 cm at the top of the basin for swelling. Steam large pudding 6 hours first day and 3 hours on day to be eaten; half-size puddings, 4 hours first day, 1½ hours on day of eating.

Serves 8–10

COLLEGE PUDDING

INGREDIENTS

1 tablespoon jam
1 cup self-raising flour
Pinch salt
¼ cup butter or clarified fat
or margarine
¼ cup sugar
1 egg
3 tablespoons milk
4 drops vanilla essence

METHOD

1. Place a saucepan of water on to boil, over which the pudding is to steam.

2. Grease a mould with butter, and put the jam in the bottom of it.

3. Cut a piece of greaseproof paper or foil the same shape as the top of the mould, but 3 cm larger than it all round.

4. Sift the flour and salt.

5. Beat the butter and sugar to a cream.

6. Beat the egg and add it gradually to the butter and sugar, beating well.

7. Stir in the milk and the vanilla.

8. Stir in the flour lightly.

9. Pour the mixture into the mould, and cover with the greased paper or foil.

10. Place in the steamer and steam for 1½ hours.

11. Turn out of the mould onto a hot dish, and serve with jam or white sauce.

VARIATIONS

GOLDEN TOP PUDDING Omit jam and replace with 2 tablespoons of honey or golden syrup.

CHOCOLATE PUDDING Omit jam and add 1 tablespoon of cocoa to the flour and 1 extra tablespoon of milk.

ORANGE OR LEMON PUDDING Omit jam and add 1 teaspoon of grated orange or lemon rind and 1 teaspoon of juice to the mixture.

FRUIT PUDDING Add ½ cup dates or sultanas or currants.

Serves 4–6

EGGLESS PUDDING

An eggless, sugarless pudding

INGREDIENTS

1 tablespoon margarine
¼ teaspoon bicarbonate of soda
2 tablespoons golden syrup
½ cup milk
1 cup self-raising flour
¼ teaspoon mixed spice

METHOD

1. Melt margarine in a basin standing in hot water.

2. Dissolve the bicarbonate of soda and golden syrup in milk and add to margarine.

3. Sift flour and spice.

4. Stir into above mixture until a smooth consistency.

5. Place into greased moulds.

6. Cover with greased paper.

7. Steam for 1 hour.

Note: This mixture is sufficient for 4. Cocoa, sultanas, dates, etc. may be added for variety.

Serves 4

STEAMED JAM ROLY

INGREDIENTS

1 ½ cups self-raising flour
Pinch salt
¼ cup butter or clarified fat or margarine
3 tablespoons water or milk
Jam

METHOD

1. Place a saucepan of water on to boil, over which the pudding is to steam.

2. Grease a pudding basin, and have a piece of greaseproof paper or foil cut a little larger than the top of the basin.

3. Sift the flour and salt.

4. Rub in the butter with the tips of the fingers.

5. Mix into a stiff dough with the water or milk.

6. Lift onto a floured board and press into a round shape.

7. Roll out 5 mm thickness and spread with jam to within 3 cm of the edge all round.

8. Roll up lightly.

9. Place into the prepared basin.

10. Cover with the paper or foil.

11. Steam for 1½ hours.

12. Turn out onto a hot plate.

13. Serve with custard or cream.

Serves 4–6

URNEY PUDDING

INGREDIENTS

1 cup plain flour
Pinch salt
¼ cup butter or margarine or dripping
¼ cup sugar
1 egg
3 tablespoons milk
½ teaspoon bicarbonate of soda
1 tablespoon jam

METHOD

1. Place a saucepan of water on to boil, over which the pudding is to steam.

2. Grease a pudding mould with butter.

3. Cut a piece of greaseproof paper or foil the same shape as the top of the mould but 3 cm larger all round.

4. Sift the flour and salt.

5. Beat the butter and sugar to a cream in a basin.

6. Beat the egg, add to butter and sugar, and beat well.

7. Stir in the milk, soda and jam.

8. Stir in the sifted flour.

9. Turn into the mould and cover with the paper or foil.

10. Steam for 1½ hours.

11. Turn out of the mould onto a hot plate and serve with stirred custard (see p. 114).

GINGER PUDDING
Substitute golden syrup for jam and add 3 teaspoons of ground ginger with the flour.

Serves 4–6

SUMMER PUDDINGS

APPLE SNOW

INGREDIENTS

4 cooking apples
2 tablespoons sugar
2 cloves
Small piece lemon rind
Cochineal
2 tablespoons water
1 or 2 egg whites

METHOD

1. Peel, core and slice apples thinly.

2. Place them in a saucepan with the sugar, cloves, lemon rind, cochineal and water.

3. Stew gently until the apples are quite tender. Drain well.

4. Beat to a pulp.

5. Beat up the egg whites to a stiff froth.

6. Add gradually to apple pulp, beating well until white and spongy.

7. Chill.

8. Serve with stirred custard (see p. 114), which may be made from the egg yolks.

Note: Pulped apricots, peaches, prunes or berries may be used instead of apple.

Serves 4

APPLE AND RICE MERINGUE

APPLE

INGREDIENTS

4 apples
2 tablespoons sugar
⅔ cup water
4 cloves

METHOD

1. Peel, core and quarter apples.

2. Boil sugar and water; add cloves and apples.

3. Cook gently with lid on until tender, then place in an ovenproof dish.

RICE

INGREDIENTS

¼ cup rice
3 cups boiling water
Pinch salt
1 egg yolk (60 g)
⅔ cup milk

METHOD

1. Place rice into a saucepan containing the boiling water and salt. Boil

for 15 minutes or until soft. Strain.

2. Return to saucepan, and add egg yolk, sugar and milk. Stir, and cook for 3 minutes.

3. Pour this mixture over the cooked apple or make it into a border.

MERINGUE

INGREDIENTS

1 egg white
Pinch salt
2 tablespoons sugar
1 teaspoon coloured sugar (see p. 247)

METHOD

1. Beat egg white stiffly, adding salt.

2. Stir in the sugar. Beat well.

3. Heap this up roughly on top of the pudding.

4. Place in a slow oven or under griller until lightly browned.

5. Sprinkle the coloured sugar over the top.

Serves 4

APPLE SPONGE

INGREDIENTS

6 cooking apples
1 cup water
4 tablespoons sugar
2 cloves

CAKE MIXTURE

2 tablespoons butter
¼ cup sugar
1 egg
⅔ cup milk
3 drops vanilla essence
1 cup self-raising flour
Pinch salt
Icing sugar

METHOD

1. Have a moderate oven in readiness.

2. Peel, quarter and core the apples.

3. Place in a saucepan with the water, 4 tablespoons sugar and cloves.

4. Cook until the apples are tender.

5. Pour into an ovenproof dish.

6. Beat the butter and ¼ cup sugar to a cream.

7. Add beaten egg gradually, and beat until the mixture thickens.

8. Add milk and vanilla.

9. Sift flour and salt, stir in lightly and quickly.

10. Pour this mixture over the hot stewed apples.

11. Bake in a moderate oven, 180°C, for about 30 minutes.

12. Sprinkle icing sugar on the top.

13. Serve with custard, cream or ice-cream.

Note: Any hot stewed or canned fruit may be used.

Serves 4–6

BAKED APRICOT PUDDING

INGREDIENTS

3 tablespoons soft white or wholemeal breadcrumbs
4 tablespoons sugar
2 cups milk
1 can (250 g) apricots or stewed apricots
3 eggs (60 g)

METHOD

1. Mix breadcrumbs and 2 tablespoons sugar.

2. Boil milk and pour onto breadcrumbs. Allow to stand for 30 minutes.

3. Grease a pie dish.

4. Place the apricots and a little of the juice (½ cup) in the pie dish.

5. Beat 3 egg yolks and 1 egg white together.

6. Add to breadcrumbs and milk, mix thoroughly, and pour onto the apricots.

7. Bake in a moderate oven, 160–180°C, until mixture sets.

8. Beat remaining egg whites stiffly, add 2 tablespoons sugar, and beat again until stiff and frothy, then pile roughly on top of pudding.

9. Return to oven for a few minutes to set white of egg.

10. Serve hot or cold.

Note: Sliced peaches or pineapple cubes may be substituted for the apricots.

Serves 4

CHOCOLATE SAUCE PUDDING

INGREDIENTS

60 g butter or margarine
½ cup sugar
1 egg (60 g)
1 cup self-raising flour
1 tablespoon cocoa
½ cup milk
Extra ½ cup sugar
Extra 1½ tablespoons cocoa
1½ cups boiling water

METHOD

1. Cream butter and sugar.

2. Add egg and beat well.

3. Fold in sifted flour and cocoa alternately with milk.

4. Place mixture into a greased ovenproof dish.

5. Mix extra sugar, cocoa and boiling water and pour over mixture.

6. Bake in a moderate oven, 180–190°C, for 35 to 40 minutes.

Note: In place of cocoa use coffee, Milo, carob or drinking chocolate.

Serves 4

BANANA CUSTARD

INGREDIENTS

2 ripe bananas
1 teaspoon lemon juice
1 quantity stirred custard (see p. 114)
Nutmeg

METHOD

1. Peel and slice bananas and sprinkle with lemon juice.

2. Place in a dish.

3. Pour custard over.

4. Grate nutmeg on top.

Serves 2

FRUIT FLUMMERY

INGREDIENTS

2 tablespoons gelatine
1 cup hot water
2 tablespoons flour
1 cup sugar
½ cup orange juice
1 tablespoon lemon juice
⅔ cup passionfruit pulp
1 or 2 egg whites (optional)

METHOD

1. Dissolve gelatine in ¼ cup hot water.

2. Blend flour with a little cold water, and carefully add to remaining hot water. Add sugar and stir over heat for 3 to 5 minutes.

3. When cooled slightly, add dissolved gelatine.

4. Add orange and lemon juice.

5. Turn into a basin and, when mixture starts to thicken, beat until very thick and foamy.

6. Add passionfruit pulp and stiffly beaten egg whites. Pour into a serving dish.

Note: Use egg yolks for stirred custard (see p. 114).

Serves 4

FRESH FRUIT SALAD

INGREDIENTS

1 small pineapple
6 passionfruit
3 peaches

2 pears
2 Kiwi fruit
3 bananas
A few strawberries
¼ cup sugar (optional)

METHOD

1. Peel the pineapple and cut finely.

2. Cut passionfruit in halves and scoop out contents.

3. Peel peaches, pears and Kiwi fruit and cut into small equal-sized pieces. Add to pineapple and passionfruit.

4. Peel bananas, cut in rings, and add with hulled strawberries to other fruit.

5. Sprinkle sugar over fruit if desired, and mix all well together.

6. Place in a salad bowl or glass dish, and let stand for 1 hour to allow a syrup to form and the flavours to blend.

7. Serve with cream or custard.

Note: Any ripe fruit may be used in a salad if carefully prepared.

Serves 6

LEMON SAUCE PUDDING

INGREDIENTS

2 eggs (60 g)
2 tablespoons butter
¾ cup sugar
2 tablespoons self-raising flour
Pinch salt
1 teaspoon grated lemon rind
⅓ cup lemon juice
1 cup milk

METHOD

1. Separate whites from yolks of eggs

2. Cream butter and sugar.

3. Add sifted flour and salt.

4. Add grated lemon rind, lemon juice, egg yolks and milk.

5. Beat egg whites until stiff, and fold into mixture.

6. Pour into a greased ovenproof dish, and stand in a dish of cold water.

7. Bake in a moderate oven, 180–200°C, for 40 minutes.

Serves 4

TRIFLE

INGREDIENTS

1 packet sponge rollettes
Double quantity Stirred
Custard (2) (see p. 114)
1 cup diced preserved pears
1 tablespoon syrup mixed with
1 tablespoon orange juice or
sherry
½ cup chopped red jelly
½ cup chopped nuts
1 cup whipped cream

METHOD

1. Slice sponge rollettes and arrange in a serving dish.

2. Sprinkle with juice and arrange fruit on top.

3. Cover the whole with custard and stand to settle.

4. Decorate with jelly, cream and nuts.

Note: If using leftover sponge cake, break into pieces and sprinkle with a mixture of 1 tablespoon each of jam, juice or sherry, then fruit. Cover with warm custard and chill before decorating.

Serves 6–8

SUMMER PUDDING

INGREDIENTS

800 g soft berry fruit
100 g sugar or according to
the sweetness of the fruit
½–1 cup water
6–8 slices white bread, crusts
removed and cut into 2–3 cm
strips

METHOD

1. Prepare fruit and place into saucepan with water and sugar. Cover.

2. Cook until fruit is soft.

3. Line the base and sides of a greased 3 cup basin or soufflé dish with bread strips.

4. Pour fruit into basin and cover top with bread strips.

5. Cover basin with a plate and put a weight on top.

6. Refrigerate overnight.

7. Turn pudding onto serving dish and coat with custard or fruit puree.

8. Decorate with sprigs of mint and serve with whipped cream.

Serves 6

LEMON SAGO

INGREDIENTS

⅓ cup sago
2 cups water
Pinch salt
1 teaspoon grated lemon rind
2 tablespoons lemon juice
1 tablespoon golden syrup
2 tablespoons brown sugar

METHOD

1. Wash sago; soak for 1 hour in the water.

2. Drain off water into saucepan, and put on to boil with pinch of salt.

3. When boiling, add the sago and stir until quite transparent.

4. Add lemon rind and lemon juice, also syrup and sugar.

5. Pour into wetted moulds and chill.

6. Turn out when set.

7. Serve with stirred custard (see p. 114).

Serves 2

LEMON SORBET

INGREDIENTS

4 cups water
2 cups sugar
1 cup strained lemon juice
1 tablespoon finely grated lemon rind (if desired)

METHOD

1. Bring water and sugar to boil, stirring to dissolve sugar, and boil for 5 minutes.

2. Cool syrup, add lemon juice and rind.

3. Pour into refrigerated trays, freeze until syrup becomes mushy.

4. Beat well and freeze again until solid.

5. Serve in chilled glass dishes.

Serves 6

VANILLA ICE-CREAM

INGREDIENTS

1 teaspoon gelatine
1 tablespoon hot water
3 cups milk
4 tablespoons full-cream
powdered milk
1 400 g tin sweetened
condensed milk
1 teaspoon vanilla essence

METHOD

1. Dissolve gelatine in hot water.

2. Beat the milk ingredients together until well blended.

3. Mix in gelatine.

4. Pour into freezer tray. Freeze for 4 hours.

5. Take out, break-up, add vanilla and beat with an electric mixer until doubled.

6. Return to freezer trays.

7. Cover with film or waxed paper. Remove from freezer 5 minutes before serving.

STRAWBERRY MOUSSE

INGREDIENTS

1 punnet strawberries
2 teaspoons hot water
2 teaspoons gelatine
2 egg whites
⅓ cup castor sugar
300 ml carton thickened
cream
1 tablespoon lemon juice

METHOD

1. Wash and hull strawberries, mash with a fork or electric blender.

2. Add gelatine to hot water, dissolve.

3. Beat egg whites until soft peaks form, gradually add sugar.

4. Whip cream and fold into egg white mixture.

5. Add strawberries, lemon juice and dissolved gelatine, *fold gently.*

6. Pour into prepared mould or individual dishes.

7. Chill until set.

Serves 4

PEACH MELBA

INGREDIENTS

2 firm, ripe peaches
150 ml pureed raspberries
Vanilla ice-cream
2 tablespoons sugar
100 ml water
¼ teaspoon vanilla

METHOD

1. Place peaches into boiling water for 30 seconds.

2. Rub skin off peaches, cut in halves and remove stone.

3. Place sugar and water in a saucepan and stir over a low heat until sugar dissolves. Boil for 3 minutes.

4. Add vanilla to syrup.

5. Poach peaches in syrup until tender.

6. Remove peaches from syrup and drain.

7. Place a scoop of ice-cream into 4 sweet dishes and cover with a peach half.

8. Coat with raspberry puree and serve at once.

9. Decorate with a rose of whipped cream.

Note: Canned peach halves may be used in place of fresh peaches.

Serves 4

RICH FRUIT ICE-CREAM

INGREDIENTS

300 ml carton cream
2 tablespoons castor sugar
2 egg whites
Pinch salt
1 cup pulped or chopped strawberries or raspberries or well-drained preserved fruit

METHOD

1. Whip cream and sugar.

2. Beat egg white and salt until stiff.

3. Combine the two.

4. Fold in fruit with 1 teaspoon essence or liqueur.

5. Pour into freezer trays and cover with film or waxed paper. Freeze for 12 hours.

CHOCOLATE ICE-CREAM

METHOD

Follow method for vanilla ice-cream: Mix 2 tablespoons cocoa with gelatine and 2 tablespoons hot water. Fold choc bits in after second beating.

APRICOT FOOL

INGREDIENTS

400 g apricot halves (pureed)
1 teaspoon lemon juice
¼ teaspoon ginger
¾ cup cream (whipped)
Nuts, chopped

METHOD

1. Mix apricot puree well with lemon juice and ginger.

2. Fold ⅔ cup whipped cream through apricot mix.

3. Spoon into glasses and chill before serving.

4. Decorate with cream and nuts.

Serves 4

CARAMEL BANANAS

INGREDIENTS

4 bananas
1 tablespoon lemon juice
60 g butter
¾ cup brown sugar

METHOD

1. Peel bananas, cut in half lengthwise then again crosswise.

2. Place into a greased pie dish and sprinkle with lemon juice.

3. Melt butter in a saucepan, add sugar and stir until sugar dissolves. Simmer for 1 minute.

4. Pour sauce over bananas.

5. Bake in a moderately hot oven, 200°C, for 8 to 10 minutes or until bananas are tender. Do not overcook.

6. Serve with cream or ice-cream, if desired.

Note: Other soft fruits may also be used in this recipe.

Serves 4–6

FRUITS—STEWED AND CASSEROLED

IN GENERAL: Fruit should retain its shape while cooking. Choose saucepan large enough for quantity of fruit. If packed too high fruit will cook unevenly and break. The quantity of sugar will vary according to personal taste. Simmer gently in a small quantity of liquid with the lid fitted tightly on the saucepan. After removing the fruit, syrup may be thickened with a little blended arrowroot or soaked sago. It may be boiled quickly without the lid for a few minutes to reduce the quantity.

CASSEROLED FRUIT

INGREDIENTS

4 apples or pears or peaches or apricots or plums or nectarines
2 tablespoons sugar
3 passionfruit

METHOD

1. Heat oven.

2. Peel, quarter and core the fruit.

3. Place peeled side up in the casserole dish, and add sugar and 1 cm of water.

4. Cover with the lid and bake very slowly, 150–160°C, until soft—about 1 hour.

5. Serve with passionfruit pulp on top of the fruit.

Serves 4

CASSEROLED RHUBARB

STEWED RHUBARB

INGREDIENTS

1 tablespoon sago
1 bunch rhubarb
¾ cup sugar
A little grated lemon rind

METHOD

1. Soak the sago in 1 cm of water in a casserole dish overnight.

2. Wash and dry the rhubarb and cut it into pieces 3 cm long.

3. Place in the casserole with the sugar and lemon rind.

4. Cover with lid and bake very slowly for 1 hour or until tender.

5. Cool and serve.

Serves 6

INGREDIENTS

1 bunch rhubarb
¼ cup water
4 tablespoons sugar
1 pinch ground ginger or 1 teaspoon lemon juice

METHOD

1. Cut the leaves off the rhubarb and trim ends of stalks.

2. Wash well.

3. Cut the stalks into pieces about 3 cm long.

4. Put water, sugar and ginger or lemon juice on to boil.

5. When boiling, add rhubarb.

6. Cook gently with the lid on until tender, about 10 to 15 minutes.

7. Allow to cool.

Serves 6

APPLE DELIGHT

INGREDIENTS

1 apple
1 tablespoon sugar
1 slice sponge cake
1 egg (60 g)

METHOD

1. Wash and dry apple.

2. Remove the core, using an apple corer or pointed knife.

3. Place on an ovenproof dish with a little water, and bake until soft.

4. Scrape out the pulp with a spoon.

5. Add sugar to the pulp.

6. Crumble the cake into crumbs.

7. Add to the apple pulp.

8. Beat the egg and stir it in.

9. Put into a saucepan and stir briskly over heat until hot—it must not boil.

10. Arrange on a dish, and serve hot or cold with stirred custard (see p. 114).

Note: Apples may be stewed instead of baked.

Serves 1

STEWED QUINCES

INGREDIENTS

2 large quinces
½ cup sugar

METHOD

1. Wash and dry quinces, peel thinly, quarter, core and slice.

2. Place into a basin of cold water to keep their colour.

3. Put 5–7 cm of water in a saucepan, add sugar and bring to boil.

4. Add the quinces and cook gently until they are quite soft and beginning to turn pink.

5. Allow to cool.

Note: Using a pressure cooker, cook at pressure for 5 minutes, cool slowly.

Serves 3–4

STEWED FRUIT

INGREDIENTS

4 cooking apples, pears,
peaches, apricots, plums or
nectarines
2 tablespoons sugar
2 cloves, a strip of lemon peel
or cardamon seeds

METHOD

1. Peel the fruit very thinly
if desired, cut in quarters
and remove the cores.

2. Put 1–2 cm of water in a
saucepan, add sugar and
cloves and bring to boil.

3. When boiling, add the
fruit.

4. Cook gently with the lid
on until tender.

5. Allow to cool, remove
the cloves or peel.

Serves 4

BAKED APPLE

INGREDIENTS

1 apple
1 teaspoon sugar
1 clove
A little butter
Icing sugar

METHOD

1. Wash and dry apple.

2. Remove the core a little
more than halfway through
from the flower end.

3. Fill up this hole with the
sugar, clove and butter.

4. Slit the skin around the
centre to prevent the apple
from bursting.

5. Place it in a small pie
dish with just a little water
in the bottom to prevent it
from sticking.

6. Bake in moderate oven,
180–200°C, for 30 minutes
or until tender.

7. Serve on a small plate
with remaining syrup.
Sprinkle with icing sugar.

Serve 1 apple per person

STEWED DRIED APRICOTS

INGREDIENTS

250 g dried apricots
2 cups water
2 tablespoons sugar

METHOD

1. Wash apricots.

2. Soak in cold water until soft.

3. Place soaked apricots and water and sugar into a saucepan.

4. Bring to the boil, simmer gently with lid on for 10 minutes or until tender.

5. Serve hot or cold with milk pudding, ice-cream or yoghurt.

Note: Prunes, peaches, nectarines, pears and apples may be cooked in the same manner.

Serves 4

BATTERS

BATTER FOR FISH, MEAT OR SAVOURY DISHES

INGREDIENTS

1 cup plain flour
Pinch salt
1 egg yolk
⅔ cup milk

METHOD

1. Sift flour and salt.

2. Make a well in the centre.

3. Pour in egg yolk.

4. Stir lightly.

5. Add milk gradually.

6. Beat well to make batter smooth and light.

7. Allow to stand about 30 minutes before using.

Note: 1 tablespoon of mayonnaise may be added to enhance the flavour.

ECONOMICAL BATTER

INGREDIENTS

1 cup self-raising flour
Pinch salt
⅔ cup milk

METHOD

1. Sift flour and salt.

2. Make a well in middle of flour.

3. Add milk gradually and mix with wooden spoon until smooth.

144

FRITTER BATTER

INGREDIENTS

1 cup self-raising flour
Pinch salt
1 tablespoon melted butter or oil
⅔ cup tepid water (2 parts cold, 1 part boiling)
1 egg white

METHOD

1. Sift flour and salt into a basin

2. Make a well in the middle.

3. Pour in oil or butter.

4. Stir flour in gradually with back of a wooden spoon.

5. Add water, a little at a time.

6. Beat into a smooth batter.

7. Beat egg white stiffly.

8. Stir it in very lightly last of all, just before using.

Note: This may be used for all kinds of fruit fritters. Add 1 tablespoon castor sugar for sweet batter.

BATTER FOR PANCAKES, ETC.

INGREDIENTS

1 cup plain flour or ½ cup plain white flour and ½ cup wholemeal self-raising flour
Pinch salt
1 egg
1¼ cups milk

METHOD

1. Sift flour and salt and make a well in the middle.

2. Break egg into the well and stir in some flour from the sides.

3. Add milk, a little at a time. When half the milk is used, all the flour must be moistened.

4. Beat well to remove all lumps and make light.

5. When quite smooth, add the remainder of the milk gradually.

6. Stand for 1 hour.

Note: This batter may also be used for Yorkshire pudding and sausages in batter.

PANCAKES

INGREDIENTS

Pancake batter (see p. 145)
1½ tablespoons butter
1 lemon
1 tablespoon sugar

METHOD

1. Measure carefully 2 tablespoons of batter into a mug or cup.

2. Prepare a small pan as follows: put a small piece of butter or fat in the pan, burn it and wipe quite dry with a small piece of kitchen paper, put another small piece of butter in pan, melt it.

3. Pour measured amount of batter into the pan, and allow it to spread evenly by tilting the pan.

4. Cook quickly until set and slightly brown.

5. Loosen edges with a knife or spatula.

6. Toss or turn pancake and cook on other side until brown.

7. Stand on a warm plate.

8. Melt a little more butter in pan, measure batter, and pour in as before.

9. While this is setting, sprinkle lemon juice and sugar on cooked pancake, roll, and put on a plate. Keep hot over a saucepan of boiling water, to prevent drying.

10. Serve as soon as possible on a hot dish, with thin slices of lemon, and sugar sprinkled over.

Note: Jam or savoury fillings may be used instead of lemon and sugar (see *Commonsense Cookery Book* 2, p. 124).

Serves 4–6

PIKELETS

INGREDIENTS

*1 cup self-raising flour (white
or wholemeal)
Pinch salt
¼ teaspoon bicarbonate of
soda
1 egg
½ cup sour milk, or fresh
milk plus 1 teaspoon lemon
juice or vinegar, or ¾ cup
milk if wholemeal flour is
used.
2 tablespoons sugar
2 teaspoons melted butter or
oil*

METHOD

1. Sift flour, salt and soda.

2. Place egg, milk, sugar
and butter in centre of
flour.

3. Beat until smooth and a
thick pouring consistency.

4. Place by dessertspoonful
onto heated and greased
griddle iron or electric pan.

5. Cook until bubbles
show.

6. Turn with a spatula and
cook until lightly brown.

7. Cool on cloth or
between layers of paper
towel.

Makes about 24

BANANA FRITTERS

INGREDIENTS

*4 bananas
1 quantity fritter batter (see
p. 145)
Frying fat or oil
Icing sugar*

METHOD

1. Peel bananas and cut
into 4 pieces.

2. Add bananas to fritter
batter, mix in very lightly.

3. Deep-fry a golden brown
colour.

4. Drain on absorbent
paper.

5. Serve on a hot dish or
plate. Sprinkle with icing
sugar.

Serves 4

YORKSHIRE PUDDING

INGREDIENTS

Pancake batter (see p. 145)
2 tablespoons clarified fat

METHOD

1. Heat clarified fat in a
cake pan, baking dish or
patty pans.

2. Pour batter in.

3. Bake in a moderate
oven, 180–190°C, for 20 to
30 minutes according to
thickness.

4. If cooked in a baking
dish drain the fat out of the
pan; cut pudding into
triangles or squares.

5. Serve as an
accompaniment to roast
beef.

Note: If meat is placed on a
trivet, the mixture can be
cooked in the baking dish
under the meat.

PASTRY

FLAKY PASTRY

INGREDIENTS

1 cup plain flour
½ teaspoon baking powder
⅛ teaspoon salt
60 g clarified fat, lard or margarine
3 tablespoons water

METHOD

1. Sift the flour, baking powder and salt.

2. Soften the fat, and divide into four.

3. Rub one fourth into the flour.

4. Add the water nearly all at once, adding a little more water if necessary to make into a dough the same consistency as the fat.

5. Turn onto a slightly floured board.

6. Knead until smooth.

7. Roll out, into a thin rectangular shape.

8. Spread another fourth of the fat on the top of ⅔ of the pastry, leaving a margin about 2 cm wide all round the edge of the dough.

9. Sprinkle lightly with flour.

10. Fold in three even folds, from the bottom, and press the edges well together.

11. Turn the dough so that an open end faces you.

12. Roll out straight from you.

13. Repeat steps 8–12 twice.

14. Roll to size and shape required.

CHOUX PASTRY

Note: Choux pastry may be used for savoury and sweet puffs and eclairs.

Makes about 24

INGREDIENTS

¼ cup butter
1¼ cups water
1 cup plain flour
3 eggs (60 g)

METHOD

1. Grease scone tray.

2. Boil butter and water in a saucepan.

3. Remove from stove, stir in sifted flour all at once and beat until smooth.

4. Beat well over heat and cook until it leaves the sides of the saucepan (do not undercook).

5. Allow to cool slightly (no more than 5 minutes).

6. Add eggs one at a time beating well after each addition.

7. Shape as required using a spoon or forcing bag.

8. Bake in a hot oven, 220–250°C, for 30 minutes in gradually decreasing heat.

9. Do not open oven door for at least 10 minutes.

SHORTCRUST PASTRY

INGREDIENTS

1 cup plain flour and ½ teaspoon baking powder or ½ cup plain flour and ½ cup self-raising flour
¼ teaspoon salt
60 g clarified fat, lard, margarine or butter
2 tablespoons water

METHOD

1. Sift dry ingredients.

2. Rub in the fat with the tips of the fingers until the mixture looks like breadcrumbs, lifting it well out of the basin during the process to admit the air.

3. Add the water gradually, making into a very dry dough. Do not add all the water unless necessary.

4. Turn onto a lightly floured board.

5. Roll to shape and size required.

PUFF PASTRY

INGREDIENTS

250 g butter
2 cups or 250 g plain flour
⅛ teaspoon salt
Squeeze of lemon juice
⅔ cup iced water

METHOD

1. Make butter into an oblong pat about 2.5 cm thick and put in refrigerator.

2. Sift the flour and salt.

3. Mix water and lemon juice together, and add to flour.

4. Make into a soft but not sticky dough, and turn onto a floured board.

5. Knead lightly and roll out square about 1 cm thick.

6. Put the pat of butter on one side of the pastry.

7. Wet round the edge of the pastry, fold over the butter, and press edges together.

8. Turn the pastry so that the fold is at the right-hand side, and roll the pastry out into a thin sheet, rolling from you only. Do not turn pastry over.

9. Sprinkle with flour, fold in three, turn so that an open end faces you, and roll out from you only.

10. Fold and put aside in refrigerator for 10 minutes.

11. Repeat until the pastry has been folded four times.

12. Roll to the shape and size required.

SUET CRUST

INGREDIENTS

60 g suet
1 cup self-raising flour
⅛ teaspoon salt
2 tablespoons water or milk

METHOD

1. Skin, flake, and grate or chop suet very finely.

2. Sift flour and salt.

3. Add suet; rub well into flour with tips of fingers.

4. Add water gradually, making a very dry dough. Do not add all water unless necessary.

5. Put pastry on a floured board.

6. Knead slightly until smooth.

7. Roll out to size and shape required.

Note: Packeted prepared suet is available. Suet crust is best steamed or boiled.

BISCUIT PASTRY

INGREDIENTS

125 g butter
½ cup sugar
½ cup self-raising flour
1½ cups plain flour
1 egg

METHOD

1. Cream butter and sugar.

2. Add egg and beat well.

3. Add sifted flours.

4. Knead lightly.

5. Roll out to size and shape required.

6. Bake in a moderate oven, 180°C, for approximately 20 minutes.

CHOCOLATE ECLAIRS

INGREDIENTS

1 quantity choux pastry (see p. 150)
300 ml cream
1 quantity chocolate warm icing (see p. 188)

METHOD

1. Force pastry mixture through bag and plain pipe in 5 cm lengths onto greased pan.

2. Bake in a moderately hot oven, 200–300°C, for 30 minutes. Do not open oven door for at least 10 minutes.

3. When cold make an incision in one side and fill with sweetened and flavoured whipped cream.

4. Cover with chocolate icing.

Makes 12

pastry onto pan, allowing room to spread.

3. Bake in a hot oven, 220–250°C, for 30 minutes or longer, gradually decreasing heat. Do not open oven door for at least 10 minutes.

4. When cooked, cool on a cooler.

5. When cool, open near the top.

6. Fill with whipped cream or custard.

7. Sprinkle with icing sugar.

Makes 18–24

CREAM OR CUSTARD PUFFS

INGREDIENTS

1 quantity choux pastry (see p. 150)
Cream or custard (see p. 154)
Icing sugar

METHOD

1. Grease scone tray.
2. Place small spoonfuls of

CUSTARD FOR PUFFS

INGREDIENTS

2 tablespoons butter
2 tablespoons plain flour
1¼ cups milk
2 egg yolks (60 g)
1½ tablespoons sugar
Vanilla to taste

METHOD

1. Melt butter.

2. Add flour and beat smooth.

3. Cook well for 2 minutes.

4. Add milk; stir until boiling.

5. Remove from heat.

6. Beat and add egg yolks.

7. Add sugar.

8. Return to heat and cook for a minute without boiling, stirring continually.

9. Add vanilla.

10. Cool before using for filling.

BAKED APPLE PUDDING

INGREDIENTS

4 small apples
2 teaspoons butter
2 tablespoons sugar
4 cloves
1 teaspoon grated lemon rind
1 quantity shortcrust pastry
(see p. 150)
Water and sugar for glazing
Icing sugar

METHOD

1. Have a hot oven in readiness.

2. Peel each apple, thinly; remove core without breaking fruit.

3. Fill up the hole with a little butter, sugar and a clove and lemon rind.

4. Cut pastry into four equal parts.

5. Roll each part into a square large enough to cover the apple.

6. Place an apple on each piece, gather edge of pastry over top of apple and pinch edges together.

7. Glaze with water and sugar and place on a slide.

8. Place in hot oven, 220–230°C, and cook for 30 minutes, gradually decreasing the heat.

9. Test with skewer; if cooked, apple is soft.

10. Lift onto suitable dish, sprinkle with icing sugar, and serve hot or cold with cream, custard or yoghurt.

Serves 4

BUTTERSCOTCH PIE

INGREDIENTS

1 quantity biscuit pastry or crumb crust (see p. 152)
3 tablespoons maize cornflour
¾ cup milk
2 tablespoons butter
¾ cup brown sugar
2 eggs
¼ teaspoon vanilla
4 tablespoons white sugar

METHOD

1. Line a tart plate with prepared pastry, prick base well and bake in a moderate oven, 180°C, for 15 minutes.

2. Blend cornflour with a little of the milk.

3. Heat butter, brown sugar and milk in a saucepan (do not boil).

4. Separate yolks from whites of eggs.

5. Stir blended cornflour into milk and bring to boil.

6. Combine beaten yolks with heated cornflour mixture. Stir in vanilla.

7. Pour into cooked pastry shell.

8. Beat egg whites until stiff, then gradually add sugar and beat until thick.

9. Pile roughly on top of pie and cook in a moderate oven, 160°C, until pale brown and firm.

Serves 4

CUSTARD TART

INGREDIENTS

2 eggs (60g)
2 tablespoons sugar
1 ¼ cups milk
3 drops vanilla essence
1 quantity shortcrust pastry
(see p. 150)
1 tablespoon jam
Nutmeg

METHOD

1. Break eggs. Set aside a little of the white from one egg.

2. Beat eggs and sugar; then add the milk and vanilla.

3. Roll out pastry 2 cm larger than 18 cm × 3 cm tart plate or foil pan.

4. Place plate on pastry, and cut round with a sharp knife.

5. Wet edge of plate, and place pastry strips on with cut side out. Glaze, cover with large piece of pastry, and trim edge.

6. Ornament round the edge, and brush the edge and bottom with the remaining egg white.

7. Spread with jam.

8. Fill centre with the custard—pour in slowly.

9. Sprinkle nutmeg on top.

10. Bake in a hot oven, 230°C, for 10 minutes; reduce to 180°C and cook for 20 minutes or until the custard is set.

Serves 4

QUICKLY MADE LEMON CHEESE TART

INGREDIENTS

½ quantity biscuit pastry (see p. 152)
1 tablespoon butter
¾ cup sugar
1 egg
Juice and rind of 1 large lemon

METHOD

1. Line an 18 cm × 3 cm tart plate or an 18 cm × 3 cm foil pan with pastry.

2. Cream butter and sugar.

3. Add egg, lemon rind and juice; beat well.

4. Pour into uncooked pastry shell.

5. Bake in a moderate oven, 180–200°C, for 20 to 30 minutes.

Serves 4

MINCE TART

INGREDIENTS

⅓ cup sultanas
⅓ cup currants
1 tablespoon candied peel
2 large apples
⅓ cup brown sugar
1 tablespoon butter
⅛ teaspoon nutmeg
A little grated lemon rind and juice
⅛ teaspoon spice
Double quantity shortcrust pastry (see p. 150)
Egg white or water and sugar for glazing
Icing sugar

METHOD

1. Wash and dry fruit.

2. Cut peel finely.

3. Peel, quarter and core apples; cut into dice or grate.

4. Mix fruits, sugar, butter and flavourings together.

5. Divide shortcrust into two, one piece a little larger than the other.

6. Roll the larger piece out a little larger than the tart plate.

7. Line the plate with pastry.

8. Wet round the edge, and put fruit mixture in.

9. Roll out the remainder of the pastry.

10. Cover the fruit.

11. Trim pastry, firming edges together.

12. Glaze with white of egg or water and sugar.

13. Bake in a hot oven, 220–230°C, for 15 minutes.

14. Reduce heat and cook for 30 minutes longer.

15. Sift icing sugar over top before serving.

Serves 4

APPLE PIE

INGREDIENTS

4–6 cooking apples
2 tablespoons sugar
2 cloves
*1 quantity flaky pastry or
shortcrust pastry (see pp. 149,
150)*
*Egg white or water and sugar
for glazing*
Icing sugar

METHOD

1. Peel, quarter and core
the apples.

2. Slice into a pie dish; add
sugar, cloves and grated
rind in layers. (If using
shortcrust pastry, cook fruit
before putting into pie
dish.)

3. Heap up well towards
the centre or use a pie
funnel.

4. Roll out pastry in the
shape of the pie dish,
2.5 cm larger.

5. Cut a strip off all round.

6. Wet the edge of the dish
and put the strip on, the cut
edge outward.

7. Brush with water, and
put the remainder of the
pastry on.

8. Trim the edges, using a
sharp knife, cutting from
you.

9. Make an incision in the
top of pastry to allow steam
to escape.

10. Glaze by brushing with
white of egg or with water
and sugar.

11. Bake in a hot oven,
220–260°C, until brown—
about 20 minutes. If
uncooked apples have been
used, reduce temperature
after 20 minutes and cook
until they are soft.

12. Sprinkle with icing
sugar and serve.

Note: Rhubarb, blackberries,
peaches or apricots can be
substituted for apples.

Serves 3–4

CHEESECAKE

INGREDIENTS

*1 quantity shortcrust pastry
(see p. 150)*
2 eggs
*125 g cream cheese or cottage
cheese*
¼ cup sugar
1 tablespoon plain flour
½ teaspoon vanilla essence

METHOD

1. Line an 18 cm tart plate
with pastry and bake for 15
to 20 minutes at
190–200°C.

2. Separate whites from
yolks of eggs.

3. Soften cheese by beating
well then add egg yolks,
sugar, flour and vanilla
essence. Mix well.

4. Beat whites of eggs until
stiff. Fold into mixture.

5. Put into pastry.

6. Bake in a moderate
oven, 180–200°C, until
set—approximately 30
minutes.

Serves 4–6

BAKED JAM ROLL

INGREDIENTS

*1 quantity shortcrust pastry
(see p. 150)*
Jam
1 cup water
¼ cup sugar
1 tablespoon butter

METHOD

1. Grease a deep ovenproof
dish.

2. Roll out shortcrust pastry
5 cm in thickness.

3. Wet edge of pastry with
water or milk.

4. Spread pastry with jam.

5. Roll up, press edges
together and put into dish.

6. Boil water, sugar and
butter for the sauce.

7. Pour slowly over roll.

8. Bake at 200–220°C for
about 30 minutes.

Note: Well-drained fruit or a
mixture of dried fruits and
brown sugar may be used
instead of jam.

Serves 4

LEMON MERINGUE TART

INGREDIENTS

2 tablespoons plain flour
2 tablespoons cornflour
½ cup white sugar
½ cup lemon juice
1 cup boiling water
2 egg yolks
1 tablespoon butter
Grated rind of 1 ripe lemon
1 cooked 23 cm biscuit pastry shell (see p. 152)

MERINGUE

2 egg whites
4 tablespoons sugar

METHOD

1. Blend flour, cornflour and sugar in a saucepan with the lemon juice.

2. Add boiling water and cook, stirring all the time until it thickens.

3. Add slightly beaten egg yolks, butter and lemon rind. Mix well.

4. Place in cooked pastry case.

5. Beat egg whites until stiff, add sugar gradually, and beat until thick.

6. Pile on top of filling. Place in a very moderate oven or under a slow griller and lightly brown.

Serves 4.

APPLE AND RICOTTA TART

INGREDIENTS

125 g wheatmeal biscuits
60 g margarine or butter, melted
½ teaspoon cinnamon
2 small eggs
200 g tinned pie apples
½ cup sour cream
Juice and rind of ½ lemon
½ cup ricotta cheese
2 teaspoons brown sugar

METHOD

1. Preheat oven to 180°C.

2. Combine crushed biscuits, melted butter or margarine and cinnamon— mix well.

3. Press in square cake pan or foil pie plate.

4. Beat eggs; add apple, sour cream, lemon juice and rind, ricotta cheese and sugar.

5. Spoon filling over base.

6. Bake for 35 to 40 minutes or until set.

7. Cool and cut into slices.

Serves 4–6

SMALL TARTS

Make small pastry cases using biscuit or shortcrust pastry (see pp. 152, 150).

LEMON CHEESE

1. Cook pastry cases. Cool.

2. Fill with lemon cheese (see p. 187).

3. Whipped cream or a small meringue may be placed on each.

COCONUT

1. Place 1 teaspoon of jam in bottom of uncooked pastry cases.

2. Mix 1 cup desiccated coconut, ½ cup sugar.

3. Beat 1 egg and add to mixture.

4. Place spoonfuls into cases on top of jam and bake in moderate oven, 180°C, until golden brown—about 20 minutes.

BUTTERSCOTCH

1. Fill uncooked pastry cases with mixture for Butterscotch Pie (see p. 155).

2. Bake at 180°C until set—about 20 minutes.

3. Top with meringue mixture.

Makes about 12

CAKES

Have everything prepared and ready before commencing to mix the cake.

- *Have the shelves positioned and the oven set at the correct temperature.*
- *Have all ingredients measured.*
- *Have slides, trays or tins greased or lined with paper then proceed without interruption to make and bake the cake.*

Cake tins should have space around them. They must not touch the sides or back of the oven nor one another. If two tins will not fit on the one shelf, use two shelves close to the middle of the oven. Do not place one cake directly above the other.

Cook until the surface of the cake is dry and lightly browned. When the cake is cooked it will be well risen and slightly shrunken from the sides, and the centre top will be elastic to the touch when lightly pressed. For large butter and fruit cakes, a fine steel skewer, cake tester or clean millet straw placed through the centre comes out free of any mixture when the cake is cooked.

If a large cake is browning too quickly, place a layer of clean white or brown paper over the top.

APPLE CAKE

INGREDIENTS

CAKE

125 g butter
½ cup sugar
2 eggs (60 g)
1½ cups self-raising flour
1 cup cornflour
4 tablespoons milk

APPLE MIXTURE

3 large green skinned apples,
peeled and grated
1 tablespoon grated lemon
rind
2 tablespoons sugar

ICING

2 cups icing sugar
Lemon juice
1 small teaspoon ground
cinnamon

METHOD

1. Have a moderate oven in readiness.

2. Grease a slab cake pan 28 cm × 18 cm × 4 cm or line with greased paper.

3. Cream butter and sugar.

4. Add well-beaten eggs.

5. Stir in lightly the sifted flour and cornflour.

6. Press half the cake mixture in the prepared pan.

7. Cover with the apple mixture, previously prepared and mixed together.

8. Add milk to remainder of cake mixture and spread with a knife.

9. Bake in a moderate oven, 180–190°C, for 20 to 30 minutes.

10. When cool, cover with warm icing (see p. 188). flavoured with lemon juice.

11. Sprinkle with cinnamon.

CINNAMON CRUMBLE RING

INGREDIENTS

2 cups self-raising flour
2 tablespoons sugar
1 egg
1 cup milk
3 tablespoons margarine

TOPPING

3 tablespoons self-raising flour
3 tablespoons brown sugar
1 tablespoon margarine
2 teaspoons cinnamon

METHOD

1. Sift flour; stir in sugar.

2. Beat egg and add the milk to it.

3. Melt margarine.

4. Make a well in centre of flour and sugar and beat in egg and milk mixture.

5. Add melted margarine and mix well.

6. Pour into a well-greased 20 cm × 7 cm ring cake pan.

7. Mix all ingredients for topping until crumbly.

8. Sprinkle over cake.

9. Bake at 180–200°C for about 30 minutes.

10. Cool for 10 minutes before removing from pan.

MAIDS OF HONOUR

INGREDIENTS

1 quantity shortcrust pastry (see p. 150)
Jam
1 quantity basic plain cake mixture (see p. 181)

METHOD

1. Preheat oven.

2. Roll pastry out thinly and stamp into rounds with a fancy cutter.

3. Line patty pans with pastry rounds.

4. Put ½ teaspoon of jam in each.

5. Put a teaspoon of cake mixture into each prepared patty pan.

6. Decorate tops with strips of pastry in fancy shapes made from scraps.

7. Bake in a hot oven,
230–250°C, for 20 minutes,
gradually decreasing heat.

8. Turn onto a cake cooler
to cool.

Makes about 12

SWISS ROLL

INGREDIENTS

3 eggs (60 g)
½ cup sugar
1 cup plain flour
*½ teaspoon bicarbonate of
soda and 1 teaspoon cream of
tartar, or 2 teaspoons baking
powder*
2 tablespoons hot milk
3 tablespoons jam

METHOD

1. Preheat oven.

2. Grease a 35 cm × 25 cm
× 2 cm Swiss roll pan and
line with greased paper.

3. Beat egg whites and
yolks separately, whites
until stiff, then together.

4. Add sugar, and continue
beating until thick.

5. Stir in sifted flour, cream
of tartar and soda or baking
powder, mixing very lightly.

6. Heat milk and add to
mixture, stirring lightly.

7. Pour mixture into lined
pan.

8. Bake in a moderate
oven, 190–200°C, for about
10 minutes.

9. Turn onto paper
sprinkled with sugar.

10. Trim edges and roll
with paper.

11. Unroll.

12. Spread quickly with
jam.

13. Roll cake and place on
a cooler to cool.

CAKES

GINGER SPONGE

INGREDIENTS

1 tablespoon butter
½ cup brown sugar
1 egg (60 g)
½ cup milk
1 tablespoon treacle or golden syrup
1 cup plain flour
2 teaspoons ginger
2 teaspoons cinnamon
1 teaspoon bicarbonate of soda
Mock Cream Filling (1) (see p. 187)
Icing sugar

METHOD

1. Preheat oven.

2. Grease two 18 cm × 4 cm shallow cake pans.

3. Beat butter and sugar to a cream.

4. Beat egg well, mix the milk and treacle with it.

5. Add gradually to the creamed butter and sugar.

6. Lightly stir in the sifted flour, ginger, cinnamon and soda.

7. Pour into the prepared pans.

8. Bake at 150–180°C for about 15 minutes.

9. Turn onto a cooler to cool.

10. When cool join together with mock cream and sprinkle with icing sugar.

GINGERBREAD

INGREDIENTS

220 g plain flour
¼ teaspoon salt
¼ teaspoon bicarbonate of soda
½ small cup treacle
1 teaspoon powdered ginger
110 g brown sugar
110 g butter or margarine
2 eggs

METHOD

1. Preheat oven.

2. Prepare slab tin—18 cm × 28 cm × 3 cm.

3. Sift flour, salt and soda.

166

4. Place treacle, butter or margarine and sugar in saucepan, mix well and heat.

5. Beat eggs and add to mixture in saucepan. Mix well.

6. Fold in flour and ginger.

7. Pour into tin; bake in very moderate oven, 160°C, for 40 minutes.

8. When cooked turn onto cooler immediately.

KISS CAKES

INGREDIENTS

120 g butter
½ cup sugar
2 eggs (60 g)
1 cup plain flour
1 cup cornflour
2 teaspoons baking powder
Jam
Icing sugar

METHOD

1. Preheat oven.

2. Grease an oven slide.

3. Beat butter and sugar to a cream.

4. Add well-beaten eggs.

5. Add sifted flour, cornflour and baking powder.

6. Stir lightly, adding extra flour if necessary to make a stiff dough.

7. Put half-teaspoons of mixture on oven slide, 2 cm apart.

8. Bake at 160–180°C for about 8 minutes.

9. Turn onto a cooler.

10. When cool, join together with jam and sprinkle with icing sugar.

Makes 24

PLAIN CAKES

INGREDIENTS

60 g butter or margarine
¼ cup sugar
1 egg
4 tablespoons milk
Vanilla to taste
1 cup self-raising flour

METHOD

1. Preheat oven.

2. Grease 12-hole, deep patty pans with butter or line with paper cases.

3. Beat butter and sugar to a cream.

4. Add well-beaten egg gradually.

5. Add milk and vanilla alternately with sifted flour; stir in lightly.

6. Place mixture into patty pans or paper cases.

7. Bake in oven, 200–230°C, for about 10 minutes.

8. Turn on a cooler to cool.

Makes 12

RAINBOW CAKE

INGREDIENTS

250 g butter or margarine
1 cup sugar
3 eggs (60 g)
½ cup milk
Vanilla essence to taste
3 cups plain flour
(Self-raising flour may be used instead of plain flour and baking powder.)
2 teaspoons baking powder
A few drops red colouring
2 tablespoons cocoa blended with 2 teaspoons warm water
Jam
Icing sugar

METHOD

1. Preheat oven.

2. Grease three 18 cm × 4 cm shallow pans well with butter.

3. Beat butter and sugar until creamy.

4. Add well-beaten eggs, beat well.

5. Add milk and essence alternately with sifted flour and baking powder, mixing quickly and lightly, but do not beat.

6. Divide mixture into three equal parts.

7. Colour one part with red colouring; add blended cocoa to another part; leave the third part plain.

8. Pour each part into a different pan; smooth over with a knife.

9. Cook in a moderate oven, 180–190°C, for about 20 to 30 minutes.

10. Turn on a cooler to cool.

11. Join together with jam; brown, pink, white from bottom.

12. Sprinkle with icing sugar.

ROCK CAKES

INGREDIENTS

2 cups self-raising flour
90 g butter or margarine
¼ cup sugar
½ teaspoon ground ginger
2 tablespoons currants,
sultanas, chopped dates or
mixed fruit
1 egg (60 g)
3 tablespoons milk

METHOD

1. Preheat oven.

2. Grease an oven slide.

3. Sift flour.

4. Rub in butter lightly with tips of fingers.

5. Add sugar and ginger.

6. Add currants or sultanas, washed and dried, or chopped dates.

7. Beat egg, and add to it the milk.

8. Add egg and milk to dry ingredients, and make into a stiff dough.

9. Place mixture in small, rough heaps on prepared oven slide.

10. Bake in a hot oven, 200–230°C, for 10 to 15 minutes.

11. Allow to cool on a cake cooler.

Makes 18–24

SULTANA CAKE

INGREDIENTS

250 g butter
1 cup sugar
3 eggs
⅔ cup milk
1½ cups sultanas
3 tablespoons blanched and
chopped almonds
3 tablespoons finely sliced peel
3 cups plain flour
1½ teaspoons baking powder

METHOD

1. Preheat oven.

2. Grease an 18 cm × 7 cm
deep cake pan with butter.

3. Beat butter and sugar to
a cream.

4. Add eggs, well beaten.

5. Add milk gradually.

6. Add cleaned sultanas,
almonds and peel.

7. Add sifted flour and
baking powder.

8. Stir lightly until well
mixed.

9. Pour into the cake pan.

10. Bake at 160–180°C for
about 1½ hours.

11. Turn onto cooler to
cool.

PAVLOVA

INGREDIENTS

4 egg whites (60 g eggs)
1 cup castor sugar
½ tablespoon cornflour
1 teaspoon vinegar or lemon
juice

METHOD

1. Have eggs at room
temperature.

2. Beat egg whites until stiff
and shiny.

3. Gradually add sugar and
cornflour and beat until
thick.

4. Fold in vinegar or
lemon juice.

5. Spread with spoon or
pipe onto the prepared
paper the size and shape of
pavlova.

6. Bake in slow oven,
120–150°C, for 2 hours.

7. When cold, decorate
with fruit and cream.

LAMINGTONS

INGREDIENTS

1 quantity basic plain cake mixture (see p. 181) cooked in a slab cake pan and cut into 20 equal-sized pieces or 1 slab day-old sponge cut as above
3 cups sugar
1 cup water
⅓ cup cocoa
1 teaspoon vanilla
Desiccated coconut

METHOD

1. Put sugar and water with cocoa into saucepan.

2. Bring to boil stirring to dissolve sugar. Brush down side of saucepan with wet pastry brush.

3. Boil gently for 12 minutes without stirring.

4. Remove from heat, add vanilla and stir for 1 minute. Cool slightly.

5. Hold cakes on fork. Dip quickly. Toss in coconut.

6. Stand on rack or waxed paper to become cold and set.

Makes 20

MERINGUES

INGREDIENTS

2 egg whites (60 g)
Pinch salt
120 g crystal or castor sugar

METHOD

1. Slightly dampen greaseproof paper or aluminium foil on a flat baking tray.

2. Beat whites of eggs with salt until stiff.

3. Add sugar gradually and continue beating until thick.

4. Place in small spoonfuls on prepared tray 2 cm apart.

5. Bake in a slow oven, 120–140°C, for 1 to 1½ hours, until dry.

Makes 24 small meringues

LEMON TEACAKE

INGREDIENTS

125 g butter or margarine
¾ cup castor sugar
1 egg (60 g)
1 ¾ cups self-raising flour
½ cup milk
2 teaspoons of finely grated
lemon rind
Extra ¼ cup sugar
¼ cup lemon juice

METHOD

1. Preheat oven.
2. Grease a 25 cm × 15 cm × 6 cm loaf cake pan.
3. Cream butter and sugar.
4. Beat egg, add slowly to creamed mixture and beat well.
5. Sift flour.
6. Add alternately with milk, stirring well.
7. Fold in lemon rind.
8. Place in prepared pan.
9. Bake in a moderate oven, 180–190°C, for 30 to 35 minutes.
10. Dissolve extra sugar in lemon juice, stand in warm place.
11. When cake is cooked, remove from oven and gently spoon lemon and sugar over top.
12. Allow to remain in pan until cool.

Note: Orange rind may be used instead of lemon.

RASPBERRY BUNS

INGREDIENTS

2 cups self-raising flour
Pinch salt
60 g butter or margarine
¼ cup sugar
1 egg
4 tablespoons milk
Raspberry jam

METHOD

1. Preheat oven.
2. Grease an oven slide.
3. Sift flour and salt.
4. Rub butter in lightly.
5. Add sugar.
6. Beat egg, add to it the milk.

7. Pour egg and milk into dry ingredients.

8. Mix into a light dough.

9. Turn onto a lightly floured board.

10. Divide into twelve parts.

11. Knead each one lightly into a round shape.

12. Make a hollow in the centre of each.

13. Put in a little jam.

14. Pinch together, enclosing jam.

15. Glaze with a little milk.

16. Bake on the oven slide at 200–230°C for 15 minutes.

Makes 12

SPONGE SANDWICH

INGREDIENTS

3 eggs
¾ cup sugar
1 cup plain flour
2 teaspoons baking powder
(Self-raising flour may be used instead of plain flour and baking powder.)

3 tablespoons water
Jam or other filling
Icing sugar

METHOD

1. Preheat oven.

2. Grease two 18 cm × 4 cm shallow cake pans and dust with flour.

3. Separate egg whites from yolks.

4. Beat whites until stiff; add sugar slowly and beat well.

5. Add yolks and beat until thick.

6. Fold in sifted flour and baking powder.

7. Add water; stir lightly and quickly.

8. Pour into pans.

9. Bake in a moderate oven, 180–190°C, for 10 to 15 minutes. Cool in the pans for 5 minutes.

10. Turn onto a cake cooler or paper sprinkled with icing sugar.

11. When cool, join together with jam or suitable filling and sprinkle with icing sugar.

BOILED APPLE FRUIT CAKE

INGREDIENTS

125 g butter or margarine
1 cup sugar
1 cup water
2 medium Granny Smith apples, grated
500 g mixed fruit
1 teaspoon bicarbonate of soda
1¼ cups plain flour
1 cup self-raising flour
1 teaspoon cinnamon
1 teaspoon spice
2 eggs

METHOD

1. Prepare a 23 cm square or round tin, lined with plain and greased paper.

2. In a large saucepan boil butter, sugar, water, apple, fruit and soda for 7 minutes, stirring gently.

3. Cool completely.

4. Add sifted flour and spices and well-beaten eggs.

5. Stir until completely blended.

6. Spoon into prepared tin.

7. Bake in middle of moderate oven, 180°C, for 1 hour or until cooked when tested in centre with fine skewer or straw.

8. Cool completely in tin.

BOILED FRUIT CAKE

INGREDIENTS

1 cup water or ½ cup port wine and ½ cup water
1½ cups sultanas and 1½ cups currants or 3 cups mixed fruit
1 cup brown sugar
2 teaspoons spice
150 g butter or margarine
1 teaspoon bicarbonate of soda
2 eggs
2 cups self-raising flour (white or wholemeal)

METHOD

1. Prepare a 23 cm square or round tin lined with plain and greased paper.

2. Place liquid, fruit, sugar

and spice in a saucepan and let stand overnight.

3. Add butter and soda; bring to the boil and stir for 3 minutes.

4. Remove from heat. Allow to become cold.

5. Stir in well-beaten eggs and flour.

6. Spoon into prepared tin.

7. Bake for 65 minutes in middle of moderate oven—180°C.

8. Test in centre with straw, cake wire or fine skewer.

9. When cooked, straw should be free from cake mixture.

10. Allow to cool completely in tin.

SUGAR-FREE BANANA CAKE

INGREDIENTS

1 cup wholemeal flour
1 cup plain flour
2 teaspoons baking powder
¼ teaspoon bicarbonate of soda
½ teaspoon mixed spice
60 g butter or margarine
1 egg (60 g)
½ cup finely chopped dates
4 well-mashed ripe bananas
⅓ cup milk

METHOD

1. Preheat oven to 180°C.

2. Grease two bar pans well.

3. Sift wholemeal flour, plain flour, baking powder, soda and mixed spice into a large mixing bowl.

4. In another mixing bowl, cream butter, egg and 1 tablespoon of dry ingredients—beat well, then stir in dates and bananas.

5. Fold in remaining flour mixture alternately with milk.

6. Spread mixture in bar pans and bake for 25 to 30 minutes.

ZUCCHINI AND CARROT CAKE

Mixture makes 1.5 litre cake dish or 2 smaller cakes—16 cm × 18 cm. Cakes must have a greased glass or special mould in centre of dish.

INGREDIENTS

2 eggs
1¼ cups castor sugar
1 cup finely grated carrot
3 cups finely grated zucchini
½ cup oil
2 teaspoons vanilla essence
2 teaspoons Parisian essence

Sift together:

1 cup self-raising flour
½ cup plain flour
½ teaspooon salt
½ teaspoon bicarbonate of
soda
2 teaspoons cinnamon
½ cup chopped walnuts

METHOD—MICROWAVE

1. Prepare glass or plastic cake pans by greasing and lining with prepared paper.

2. Beat eggs until fluffy— gradually add sugar and beat until thick.

3. Pour the mixture into a large bowl, add carrot and zucchini.

4. Add oil and essences; mix well.

5. Add sifted dry ingredients and walnuts.

6. Pour mixture into a large 1.5 litre cake dish containing a centre glass.

7. Place cake dish on an upturned plate in microwave.

8. Cook on HIGH for 9 to 12 minutes.

9. Allow to cool slightly before removing from dish.

Ice with lemon icing:

2 teaspoons grated lemon rind
Juice of ½ lemon
1¼ cups sifted icing sugar
2 teaspoons melted butter

Combine to a thick consistency and spread on cake.

CHRISTMAS CAKE

INGREDIENTS

250 g raisins
250 g currants
250 g sultanas
250 g butter
1 cup sugar
1 teaspoon caramel
6 eggs (60 g)
½ cup brandy, sherry or orange juice
60 g chopped citron peel
125 g chopped dates or prunes or figs
125 g chopped almonds
2½ cups plain flour

PREPARATION

1. Clean the fruit—wash, drain and dry well the raisins, currants and sultanas or rub with plain flour.

2. Cut or chop fruits to equal-sized pieces.

3. Place in container, sprinkle with brandy, sherry or orange juice. Stir occasionally. Soak overnight.

METHOD

1. Preheat oven.

2. Line an 18 cm × 7 cm deep cake pan with 2 or 3 layers of paper or with aluminium foil.

3. Beat butter and sugar to a cream, and add caramel.

4. Add the eggs, one at a time, and continue beating.

5. Add liquid.

6. Add the prepared fruit and nuts and flour alternately, mixing well.

7. Spoon evenly into prepared pan.

8. Bake in centre of slow oven, 140–150°C, for 3 to 3½ hours.

9. Test by piercing with a skewer. If it is free from mixture when withdrawn, the cake is cooked.

10. Allow to remain in pan until cold.

11. Wrap in several layers of clean paper.

Quick Cake

INGREDIENTS

2 cups self-raising flour
2 cups sugar
4 tablespoons custard powder
1 cup milk
250 g softened margarine or
butter
1 teaspoon vanilla
4 eggs

METHOD

1. Place all ingredients in a bowl and beat with electric mixer for 10 minutes on low to medium speed.

2. Bake in two 20 cm tins 40 to 45 minutes in moderate oven, or until cooked when tested.

VARIATION

Put sliced raw apple on top of one cake and sprinkle with a mixture of cinnamon and sugar before putting it in the oven.

Honey, Fruit and Bran Muffins

INGREDIENTS

1 cup white self-raising flour
½ cup wholemeal self-raising
flour
Pinch cinnamon
¾ cup processed bran
½ cup sultanas or mixed fruit
1 egg (60 g)
¾ cup milk
2½ tablespoons honey
45 g butter
¼ teaspoon bicarbonate of
soda
¼ cup hot water

METHOD

1. Preheat oven—200°C.

2. Grease two sets of deep patty pans.

3. Sift flours and cinnamon into a bowl. Add remaining husks in sifter to flour.

4. Mix in bran and fruit.

5. Beat egg and milk together.

6. Melt honey and butter together.

7. Add soda and hot water to honey.

8. Add both liquid mixtures to flour.

9. Mix until *just* combined. Mixture should be lumpy.

10. Spoon into patty pans.

11. Bake for 20 to 25 minutes until golden brown.

Makes 24

SPICED CARROT CAKE

INGREDIENTS

4 tablespoons margarine or butter
½ cup castor sugar
1 tablespoon honey
2 eggs (60 g)
1 cup self-raising flour (white, wholemeal or a mixture of both)
1 teaspoon allspice
2 teaspoons bicarbonate of soda
1 cup grated carrot
½ cup chopped walnuts

METHOD

1. Preheat oven to 200°C.

2. Grease and line loaf tin—22 cm × 11 cm × 6½ cm.

3. Cream butter, sugar and honey.

4. Add eggs, one at a time, beat well.

5. Blend in sifted dry ingredients.

6. Add carrot and walnuts, mix well.

7. Place mixture in tin. Bake in middle of oven for 40 minutes or until cooked when tested.

8. Leave for 5 minutes. Turn onto cake cooler.

9. If desired, cover with Vienna Icing (see *Commonsense Cookery Book* 2, (p. 217) flavoured with grated lemon rind and juice.

SIMNEL CAKE

INGREDIENTS

250 g butter or margarine
1 cup brown sugar (firmly packed)
½ cup white sugar
1 tablespoon grated lemon rind
1 teaspoon vanilla
5 eggs
125 g glacé cherries, halved
250 g mixed peel
60 g chopped walnuts
60 g blanched almonds, chopped
250 g chopped sultanas
250 g chopped raisins
3 cups plain flour
1 teaspoon mixed spice
½ teaspoon baking powder
½ cup dry sherry or orange juice
375 g almond paste
Apricot jam, honey or white of egg
1 quantity boiled icing (see p. 184)

METHOD

1. Cream butter and sugar with lemon rind and vanilla.

2. Add unbeaten eggs one at a time, beating well after each addition.

3. Mix halved cherries with chopped peel, nuts, sultanas and raisins and add to creamed mixture.

4. Fold in half the sifted dry ingredients, followed by sherry or orange juice, then the remainder of the dry ingredients.

5. Place half the cake mixture into a deep 23 cm round cake tin lined with one thickness of brown paper and two thicknesses of greaseproof paper.

6. Roll out ⅓ of almond paste to 20 cm circle using cake tin as a guide.

7. Lower onto cake mixture in tin and press down well.

8. Spoon remainder of cake mixture into tin, drop tin on table a few times to level and remove air bubbles.

9. Bake in a slow oven, 150–160°C, for 3½ to 4 hours or until skewer is free from cake mixture when placed in the centre of the cake.

10. Allow to cool in tin.

11. Roll out remainder of almond paste (using a little icing sugar on board and rolling pin), trim to a round piece 1 cm larger than top of cake.

12. Brush top of cake with warmed, sieved apricot jam, honey or egg white and place almond paste on top. Flute edges with fingers.

13. From trimmings of almond paste make eleven small, egg-shaped balls.

14. Divide boiled icing into three small bowls. Leave one quantity white, colour one pale pink and the other pale green with food colouring.

15. Using a fork, dip almond eggs into boiled icing, shake to remove excess icing and place on a wire rack to dry.

16. Spoon white boiled icing onto centre of cake and spread to within 2.5 cm of cake edge.

17. Arrange eggs around edge of glaze.

Note: A nest for the eggs may be made with shredded coconut.

BASIC PLAIN CAKE

INGREDIENTS

125 g margarine or butter
¾ cup sugar
4 drops vanilla essence
2 eggs
2 cups self-raising flour
½ cup milk

METHOD

1. Grease and lightly flour desired pan (see step 5 below).

2. Cream margarine, sugar and vanilla.

3. Beat eggs and add gradually, beating well after each addition. If using an electric mixer add unbeaten eggs, one at a time, and mix each one in on medium speed.

4. Add sifted flour alternately with the milk, beginning and ending with flour. Beat 1 minute on low speed of electric mixer, or 30 strokes with a wooden spoon.

5. Spread in prepared pan. This quantity fills:

CAKES

(a)   two 18 cm shallow
cake pans
(b)   one 25 cm × 15 cm ×
6 cm loaf cake pan
(c)   two 25 cm × 9 cm ×
5 cm bar cake pans
(d)   one 18 cm × 7 cm
deep cake pan
(e)   one 28 cm × 18 cm ×
4 cm slab cake pan
(f)   one 20 cm × 7 cm ring
pan

6. Cook on centre shelf in a
moderate oven 180–190°C,
(a), (c), (e) 30 to 35 minutes;
(b), (d) and (f) 40 to 45
minutes.

7. Test if cooked by
inserting a clean thin skewer
lightly into the centre of the
cake. If it comes out free
from mixture, the cake is
cooked.

8. Stand pan on cake cooler
for 5 to 10 minutes before
turning cake out. Cool.

9. Finish as desired.

VARIATIONS

CHOCOLATE CAKE *Add 4
level tablespoons cocoa to the
flour. Increase milk by 1
tablespoon.*

ORANGE CAKE *Add
2 teaspoons grated orange
rind to sifted flour. Decrease
milk by 3 tablespoons. Add 3
tablespoons orange juice
separately from the milk.*

COCONUT CAKE *Add ½ cup
desiccated coconut before the
flour and milk.*

APPLE CAKE *Use a ring cake
pan. Top batter with very thin
slices of peeled apples. Sprinkle
with 2 teaspoons sugar and
½ teaspoon cinnamon mixed
together.*

PATTY CAKES *Spoon into
24 greased patty pans.*

SPICE CAKE *Add 1 teaspoon
ginger, ½ teaspoon cinnamon
and ½ teaspoon nutmeg to
flour. Decrease sugar to 1 cup
and add ½ cup brown sugar.*

MARBLE CAKE *Divide batter
into three in separate bowls.
Leave one plain. Add red food
colour to another. Add
2 tablespoons cocoa and
1 tablespoon milk to the third.*

*Drop alternate colours into
the prepared pan until all
batter is used. Draw a thick
skewer or thin-bladed knife in*

*circles through the batter to
streak the colours.*

CHERRY CAKE *Add 1 cup
drained cherries cut into large
pieces before adding flour.
Almond essence may be used
instead of vanilla.*

SEED CAKE *Add 1 tablespoon
caraway seeds before the flour.*

ICINGS AND FILLINGS

BOILED ICING

INGREDIENTS

2 tablespoons water
1 cup white sugar
1 egg white
Vanilla essence to taste
Colouring

METHOD

1. Put water and sugar in a saucepan and stir over heat until boiling.

2. Boil gently for 5 minutes without stirring.

3. Beat egg white to a stiff froth in a basin.

4. Pour on the boiling syrup gradually, and beat until thick.

5. Add vanilla, and, if liked, a little colouring.

6. Spread over cake.

CARAMEL ICING

INGREDIENTS

2 cups brown sugar
½ cup milk
2 tablespoons butter
¼ teaspoon vanilla

METHOD

1. Place sugar, milk and butter in a saucepan.

2. Stir over heat until boiling.

3. Boil without stirring for 5 minutes.

4. Remove from heat. Add vanilla.

5. Stir until spreading consistency and cover cake.

ALMOND PASTE OR MARZIPAN

INGREDIENTS

1 ⅓ cups icing sugar or castor sugar
1 cup ground almonds
1 egg yolk
1 tablespoon sherry or orange or lemon juice

METHOD

1. Sift sugar.

2. Add almonds, and mix well.

3. Mix into a very stiff paste with beaten yolk of egg and sherry or fruit juice.

4. Lift out onto board which has been sprinkled with icing sugar.

5. Roll out and cover cake.

Note: Cake should be brushed with egg white before covering.

VARIATION: SWEET MAKING

1. Split dessert dates and prunes and fill with small roll of mixture.

2. Mould mixture around walnuts, pecans and almonds and dust with drinking chocolate.

3. Mould into fruit and vegetable shapes, dry and tint with appropriate vegetable colours.

ORANGE OR FRUIT ICING

INGREDIENTS

1 cup icing sugar
2 tablespoons fruit juice

METHOD

1. Sift icing sugar into a bowl standing in hot water.

2. Add fruit juice and stir until smooth.

3. Pour over cake; smooth with a knife dipped in hot water if necessary.

Note: Passionfruit juice may be strained or a few seeds left in as desired. Grated rind of orange may be added to orange icing.

ROYAL ICING FOR PIPING

INGREDIENTS

1 egg white
250 g pure icing sugar
1 teaspoon strained lemon juice

METHOD

1. Sift icing sugar through a fine strainer.

2. Place egg white in medium basin, beat very lightly.

3. Add sugar gradually, mixing with wooden or plastic spoon.

4. Add lemon juice, few drops at a time.

5. Icing is ready for piping when a very small quantity pressed between thumb and forefinger leaves two straight peaks.

6. While piping onto cake, keep basin covered with a damp cloth.

7. Store any left over in airtight container in refrigerator.

8. When adding colour, drip it off a skewer or through a dropper, *one* drop at a time. Mix after each addition until desired colour is attained.

LEMON OR ORANGE FILLING FOR CAKES

INGREDIENTS

2 tablespoons arrowroot
⅔ cup water
1 tablespoon butter
1 tablespoon sugar
1 teaspoon grated lemon or orange rind
2 tablespoons lemon or orange juice

METHOD

1. Blend arrowroot with a little water.

2. Boil water and butter; add moistened arrowroot; stir and cook for 3 minutes.

3. Add sugar and grated rind and juice of fruit.

4. When cool, spread between layers of cake.

LEMON CHEESE

INGREDIENTS

1 lemon
1 egg yolk
¼ cup sugar
1½ tablespoons butter

METHOD

1. Put the grated rind and juice of the lemon into a saucepan.

2. Add the egg yolk, sugar and butter, and stir over heat until thick.

3. Allow to cool.

4. Spread between layers of cake.

Note: The whole egg may be beaten and used if liked.

MOCK CREAM FILLING (1)

INGREDIENTS

2 tablespoons butter
½ cup sifted icing sugar
½ teaspoon vanilla essence

METHOD

1. Beat butter and icing sugar to a cream.

2. Add vanilla; stir in well.

3. Spread between layers of cake.

MOCK CREAM FILLING (2)

INGREDIENTS

60 g unsalted butter
60 g sugar
1 teaspoon boiling water

METHOD

1. Cream butter and sugar until white.

2. Cover with cold water, stir, pour off water.

3. Beat well and repeat 3 or 4 times.

4. Add boiling water very gradually, beating well until light and fluffy.

Note: One tablespoon of brandy may be added to make HARD SAUCE for Christmas pudding.

WARM OR GLACÉ ICING

INGREDIENTS

1 cup icing sugar
1 tablespoon boiling water
Essence to taste
Colouring

METHOD

1. Sift the icing sugar.

2. Add boiling water gradually and mix to a thick paste. Do not add all water unless necessary.

3. Stir over boiling water until smooth consistency.

4. Add essence and colouring if required.

5. Place on cake; smooth with a knife.

VARIATIONS

CHOCOLATE ICING *Sift 1 tablespoon cocoa with icing sugar.*
COFFEE ICING *Sift 2 teaspoons coffee powder with icing sugar.*

FONDANT ICING

INGREDIENTS

500 g pure icing sugar
1 tablespoon liquid glucose
(softened over hot water)
1 egg white
Flavouring
Colouring

METHOD

1. Sift icing sugar through coffee strainer into a large basin.

2. Make a well in the centre, add softened glucose, egg white and flavouring.

3. Mix well with wooden spoon, drawing the sugar into the centre until a stiff dough-like ball is formed.

4. Turn onto a board dusted with icing sugar.

5. Knead well until quite smooth and pliable. Introduce colour one drop at a time.

COVERING THE FRUIT CAKE

1. Before rolling make sure the board is cleared of all

excess icing sugar. Rub hands and rolling pin with cornflour.

2. Have cake brushed free of crumbs, fill any hollows with fondant.

3. Brush the whole surface with lightly beaten egg white or finely sieved heated jam.

4. Stand cake on plastic sheet.

5. Roll fondant with steady even pressure to suit shape of cake—1 cm thick.

6. Place carefully on cake. Press firmly on surface.

7. Rub with hands dusted well with cornflour until surface is smooth and satiny. Avoid pressure.

8. Trim around lower edge after placing on prepared board.

9. Store the covered cake in a large airtight container or in a dry cupboard until later decoration as this icing is affected by humidity.

LIQUORICE ALLSORTS

1. Roll fondant 1 cm thick, cut into strips and press

between liquorice straps that have been brushed with egg white. Cut to required size when firm.

2. Roll fondant 1 cm thick and roll around liquorice twists. Cut to required size when firm.

FONDANT FRUITS

1. Take a quantity of large, pitted dates or prunes.

2. Split one side and insert a roll of fondant.

Note: Ready made fondant is available at cake decorating and food shops.

CREAM CHEESE ICING

INGREDIENTS

30 g butter
60 g ricotta or cream cheese
¼ teaspoon vanilla
1 cup icing sugar

METHOD

1. Soften butter.

2. Add ricotta or cream cheese and vanilla and beat until smooth.

3. Add sifted icing sugar and continue beating until smooth.

4. If the mixture is too stiff add a little milk.

Note: Substitute grated rind of one lemon for vanilla.

BISCUITS AND SLICES

To keep biscuits crisp they should be stored in Airtight *containers as soon as they are cold. Different varieties should be stored separately.*

ANZAC BISCUITS

INGREDIENTS

1 cup rolled oats
1 cup plain flour
½ cup sugar
¾ cup desiccated coconut
2 tablespoons golden syrup
½ cup butter or margarine
½ teaspoon bicarbonate of soda
1 tablespoon boiling water
Pinch salt

METHOD

1. Mix oats, flour, sugar and coconut together.

2. Melt syrup and butter together.

3. Mix soda with boiling water and add to melted butter and syrup.

4. Add to dry ingredients.

5. Place teaspoonfuls of mixture well spaced on a greased slide.

6. Bake in slow oven, 150–160°C, for 20 minutes.

Makes 50

BASIC BISCUIT RECIPE (1)—VANILLA BISCUITS

INGREDIENTS

125 g butter or margarine
½ cup sugar
¼ teaspoon vanilla
1 egg (60 g)
2 cups plain flour
1 teaspoon baking powder
Egg or milk for glazing
Pinch salt

METHOD

1. Grease pan or slide.

2. Cream butter, sugar and vanilla.

3. Beat egg and add slowly to mixture, beating well.

4. Add sifted flour and baking powder.

5. Place onto floured board, knead lightly.

6. Roll out part of the mixture at a time, keeping remainder cool.

7. Stamp out shapes with a cutter dipped in flour (4 cm round, 6 cm diamond).

8. Put on greased pan or slide.

9. Glaze with a little egg or milk.

10. Place a piece of cherry or almond on each.

11. Bake in moderate oven, 150–160°C, for about 10 minutes. The biscuits should be a very light brown when cooked.

12. Allow to cool on slide.

Note: To make a variety of biscuits from this mixture, use half as above, and prepare the other half as follows:

- Mix a small portion with chopped cherries, roll into balls and press onto greased tray.

- Roll the remainder into balls, press with a fork on greased tray, and top with pieces of ginger, grated chocolate or chocolate pieces.

Makes 36–40

BASIC BISCUIT RECIPE (2)

INGREDIENTS

1 ½ cups self-raising flour
Pinch salt
½ cup custard powder
½ cup sugar
125 g margarine or butter
3 tablespoons milk

METHOD

1. Prepare two oven slides with oven-bake paper.

2. Sift flour, salt and custard powder into bowl.

3. Add sugar.

4. Add margarine and rub in with tips of fingers until the mixture is like coarse breadcrumbs.

5. Add milk and mix very firmly by hand (a little extra milk is sometimes needed in cold weather).

6. Turn onto floured board and roll round with hand to coat lightly with flour.

7. Roll out thinly with floured rolling pin.

8. Cut into desired shapes (if a 4 cm round cutter is used, this amount makes about 48 biscuits).

9. Cook on prepared slides in a moderate oven, 150–180°C, for 12 to 15 minutes. Place one slide above the centre and one on centre rack of oven.

10. Loosen from slides with a knife while hot, as the biscuits are inclined to stick if left until cold.

VARIATIONS

CHOCOLATE COOKIES *Add 2 tablespoons cocoa to flour or add 60 g chocolate pieces, and drop dough in rough heaps. An extra teaspoon of milk may be necessary.*

CHERRY AND NUT DROPS *Add 60 g chopped cherries and 60 g chopped walnuts or peanuts. Drop in rough heaps without rolling.*

COCONUT ROUGH *Add ½ cup desiccated coconut. Drop in rough heaps.*

SPICY DATE DROPS *Add ½ teaspoon cinnamon, ¼ teaspoon nutmeg and ½ cup chopped dates. Drop in rough heaps.*

CARAMEL FINGERS

INGREDIENTS

125 g butter or margarine
¾ cup brown sugar
1 egg
½ cup chopped dates
½ cup chopped walnuts
1 cup self-raising flour
Pinch salt

METHOD

1. Grease a 28 cm × 18 cm × 4 cm slab cake pan.

2. Melt butter and sugar over slow heat.

3. Beat well and allow to cool.

4. Beat egg and add to butter and sugar.

5. Add dates, walnuts and lastly flour. Beat until smooth.

6. Press into pan.

7. Bake in moderate oven, 160–190°C, for 20 to 30 minutes.

8. Cool in pan.

9. Cut into finger lengths.

Makes 27

CINNAMON DROPS

INGREDIENTS

1½ cups plain flour
1½ teaspoons baking powder
3 teaspoons cinnamon
Little grated nutmeg
125 g butter or margarine
½ cup sugar
1 egg (60 g)
1 tablespoon milk
12 almonds, blanched and split

METHOD

1. Sift flour, baking powder, cinnamon and nutmeg.

2. Rub in butter or margarine lightly.

3. Add sugar.

4. Add well-beaten egg and milk, keeping a little for glazing.

5. Shape into small balls, rolling lightly in palms of hands.

6. Put on greased slides, brush over top with a little egg.

7. Put small piece of almond on top of each.

8. Bake in moderate oven, 150–180°C, about 10 minutes.

Note: Small portions of mixture may be moulded around a stoned date or prune.

Makes 24

CHEESE STRAWS OR BISCUITS

INGREDIENTS

¾ *cup dry cheese*
60 g butter or margarine
¾ *cup plain flour*
Salt and cayenne pepper to taste
1 egg yolk
½ *teaspoon lemon juice*

METHOD

1. Grate cheese.

2. Mix butter lightly into flour.

3. Add cheese, salt and cayenne.

4. Mix egg yolk and lemon juice, add to flour mixture, and mix to a stiff dough.

5. Roll out part of dough 5 mm thick.

6. Cut into strips 10 cm long and 5 mm wide.

7. Roll out remainder of dough, stamp into rounds with a plain cutter, and cut out centre with a smaller cutter leaving a ring.

8. Bake on greased slide in a moderate oven, 150–160°C, for 10 to 20 minutes.

9. Cool on slide.

10. To serve, fill each ring with a bundle of straws. Arrange on plate. Garnish with parsley.

Note: This mixture may be used for biscuits. Cut with a floured cutter instead of making strips and rings.

Makes 36–40

CHOCOLATE FUDGE FINGERS

INGREDIENTS

125 g butter or margarine
1 cup brown sugar
3 tablespoons cocoa or powdered chocolate
1 egg (60 g)
250 g plain sweet biscuits
1 cup mixed fruit or crushed nuts

METHOD

1. Place butter, sugar and cocoa in saucepan.

2. Stir over slow heat until butter melts and ingredients are thoroughly mixed.

3. Allow to cool.

4. Beat egg.

5. Crush biscuits to fine crumb.

6. Add egg, crushed biscuits and fruit or nuts to cooled mixture.

7. Mix well, spread into a greased 28 cm × 18 cm × 4 cm slab cake pan and place in refrigerator to set.

8. Cut into fingers.

Makes 27

CHOCOLATE COCONUT SLICE

INGREDIENTS

60 g butter or margarine
¾ cup brown sugar
1 egg (55 g or 60 g)
1 tablespoon cocoa
1 cup self-raising flour
Pinch salt
½ cup desiccated coconut

METHOD

1. Melt butter and sugar. Cool.

2. Beat in egg.

3. Sift and add cocoa, flour and salt, then add coconut. Mix thoroughly.

4. Press into a greased shallow pan 23 cm square.

5. Bake at 150–180°C for 20 to 25 minutes.

6. Mark into slices and leave in pan until cold. It may be iced with chocolate icing if desired.

Makes 24

MELTING MOMENTS

INGREDIENTS

125 g butter or margarine
2 tablespoons icing sugar
Vanilla to taste
½ cup self-raising flour
½ cup cornflour

ICING

1 tablespoon butter
1 tablespoon condensed milk
3 tablespoons icing sugar
Vanilla to taste

METHOD

1. Cream butter and sugar and vanilla.

2. Sift flour and cornflour.

3. Add to creamed mixture and mix well.

4. Roll into small balls.

5. Place on greased flat pan.

6. Bake in slow oven, 150–160°C, for 10 to 15 minutes.

7. Mix all icing ingredients together.

8. Join biscuits together with icing when cold.

Makes 12

NUTTIES

INGREDIENTS

250 g butter or margarine
1 cup sugar
1 egg
¾ cup chopped dates
¾ cup chopped walnuts
Pinch salt
2 cups plain flour
2 teaspoons cinnamon
½ teaspoon bicarbonate of soda

METHOD

1. Cream butter and sugar.

2. Add beaten egg.

3. Add dates and walnuts.

4. Add flour and cinnamon.

5. Add soda dissolved in 1 teaspoon water. Mix well.

6. Drop small spoonfuls on greased slides.

7. Bake at 150–160°C for 20 minutes.

8. Remove from slide and cool.

Makes 40

GINGER BISCUITS

INGREDIENTS

125 g margarine or butter
3 tablespoons golden syrup
3 cups self-raising flour
1 teaspoon bicarbonate of soda
1 tablespoon ground ginger
1 cup sugar
1 egg
Pinch salt

METHOD

1. Melt margarine with golden syrup on gentle heat. Cool.

2. Sift flour, soda and ginger; add sugar.

3. Beat egg and stir into margarine and syrup.

4. Add dry ingredients and mix well together.

5. Roll into balls and place on a greased slide.

6. Cook in a very moderate oven, 150–180°C, for approximately 20 minutes.

Makes 36–48

GINGER OR FRUIT SLICE

INGREDIENTS

125 g margarine or butter
½ cup brown sugar
1 teaspoon grated lemon rind
1 tablespoon golden syrup
1 egg
⅔ cup chopped ginger or crystallised pineapple and cherries
½ cup milk
1½ cups self-raising flour
1 teaspoon ground ginger

METHOD

1. Cream margarine and sugar, lemon rind, and syrup.

2. Beat egg and add gradually.

3. Add chopped ginger or fruit and milk alternately.

4. Stir in sifted flour and ground ginger.

5. Spread over the base of a well-greased 28 cm × 18 cm × 4 cm shallow slab cake pan.

6. Bake in moderate oven,

180–200°C, for 40 to 45 minutes.

7. Cool in pan.

8. Ice with lemon icing, if liked.

Makes 24

Note: For a chocolate flavour, add 2 tablespoons cocoa to mixture.

Makes 24

PEANUT BISCUITS

INGREDIENTS

125 g butter or margarine
½ cup sugar
1 egg
1¼ cups self-raising flour
Pinch salt
¾ cup raw peanuts

METHOD

1. Cream butter and sugar.

2. Add egg and beat well.

3. Mix in sifted flour and peanuts.

4. Place in small portions on a greased tray.

5. Bake at 160–190°C for 12 to 15 minutes.

6. Remove from tray and cool.

SNAP OR CRISP BISCUITS

INGREDIENTS

125 g butter
1 cup sugar
Vanilla to taste
1 egg (45 g), beaten
1 cup self-raising flour

METHOD

1. Cream butter, sugar and vanilla.

2. Add egg, beat well.

3. Sift in flour all at once. Stir until well mixed.

4. Drop small sections from spoon onto greased tray.

5. Bake at 140–160°C for 10 to 15 minutes, until golden brown.

Note: ½ teaspoon of grated lemon or orange rind may be added for variety.

Makes 18

CORNFLAKE OR RICE BUBBLE CRISPS

INGREDIENTS

2 egg whites (60 g eggs)
½ cup sugar
4 cups cornflakes or rice bubbles
Pinch salt
¾ cup chopped nuts
½ cup desiccated coconut
2 tablespoons melted butter

METHOD

1. Beat egg whites, add sugar, and beat until stiff.

2. Add dry ingredients.

3. Lastly add melted butter.

4. Place in spoonfuls on a greased slide.

5. Bake in moderate oven, 150–160°C, for 10 to 15 minutes.

6. Remove from hot slide to cool.

Makes 30

RASPBERRY SLICES

INGREDIENTS

125 g butter
½ cup sugar
2 eggs (60 g)
1½ cups self-raising flour
Pinch salt
Raspberry jam
½ cup additional sugar
1 cup desiccated coconut

METHOD

1. Cream butter and sugar.

2. Mix in 1 egg.

3. Add sifted flour. Mix well.

4. Spread thinly in flat well-greased or lined 28 cm × 18 cm × 4 cm Swiss roll pan.

5. Spread with raspberry jam.

6. Beat remaining egg and sugar together, add coconut.

7. Spread over jam.

8. Bake in a moderate oven, 180–200°C, for about 20 minutes.

9. When cold cut into slices.

Makes 24

WHEATMEAL BISCUITS

INGREDIENTS

125 g butter or margarine
½ cup sugar
1 egg (60 g)
Vanilla to taste
2 cups self-raising flour
1 cup fine wheatmeal
Pinch salt

METHOD

1. Grease an oven slide.

2. Cream butter and sugar.

3. Add egg and vanilla. Beat well.

4. Add flour and wheatmeal.

5. Divide into three equal parts.

6. Make each part into a roll about 4 cm in diameter on lightly floured board.

7. Wrap in plastic wrap or waxed paper.

8. Chill in refrigerator until firm.

9. Slice thinly. Place on greased slide.

10. Bake at 150–180°C for 10 to 15 minutes.

Makes 60

SHORTBREAD

INGREDIENTS

250 g butter or margarine
½ cup castor sugar
2 cups plain flour
½ cup rice flour
½ teaspoon baking powder

METHOD

1. Cream butter and sugar.

2. Add flours and baking powder, sifted.

3. Mix thoroughly.

4. Turn onto a lightly floured board.

5. Flatten until round, about 23 cm across, and pinch frill round edges.

6. Mark sections with back of knife.

7. Place on greased slide.

8. Bake in very moderate oven, 150°C, for 40 minutes. Do not brown.

9. Cool on slide.

REFRIGERATOR BISCUITS

INGREDIENTS

3 cups plain flour
1½ teaspoons baking powder
180 g butter or margarine
1¼ cups brown sugar
1 teaspoon vanilla essence
1 egg (60 g)
½ cup finely chopped dates
½ cup chopped cherries
½ cup chopped raisins or ginger or nuts
Pinch salt

METHOD

1. Sift flour and baking powder.

2. Cream butter, sugar and vanilla.

3. Beat egg and add to creamed mixture.

4. Add flour and mix well.

5. Divide into four equal parts. Make one section into a roll about 4 cm in diameter. Knead dates into second section and roll as above. Knead cherries into third section and roll. Knead raisins or ginger or nuts into fourth section and roll.

6. Wrap each section in plastic wrap or waxed paper.

7. Chill in refrigerator until quite firm.

8. Slice thinly. Place onto a greased slide.

9. Bake at 150–180°C for 10 to 15 minutes.

10. Cool on slide.

Makes 48

SCONE AND LOAF MIXTURES

CHEESE LOAF OR SCONES

INGREDIENTS

2 cups self-raising flour
1 tablespoon or 30 g butter or margarine
½ cup grated cheese
Pinch salt
1 egg
½ cup milk
½ cup water

METHOD

1. Sift flour.
2. Rub in butter and cheese.
3. Add salt.
4. Moisten with beaten egg, milk and water.
5. Shape into scones or place in greased loaf pan.
6. Bake loaf in a moderate oven, 200–220°C, for 40 minutes; bake scones at 220–260°C for 8 to 10 minutes.

VARIATIONS

SALAD LOAF *Add ¼ cup chopped celery and shallot and grated carrot.*

HERB AND GARLIC *Add 1 teaspoon chopped garlic, 1 tablespoon chopped fresh herbs or 1 teaspoon dried herbs and 1 tablespoon chopped parsley.*

BACON AND CORN *Add 2 rashers of bacon cooked crisp and crumbled, ¼ cup corn kernels and 1 tablespoon chopped parsley or chives.*

NUT *Add ½ cup chopped nuts.*

Makes 18

SCONES

INGREDIENTS

2 cups self-raising flour
¼ teaspoon salt
2 tablespoons or 60 g butter
or margarine
1 cup milk

METHOD 1

1. Have a hot oven in readiness.

2. Grease an oven slide.

3. Sift flour and salt.

4. Rub butter in lightly with tips of fingers.

5. Pour nearly all the milk in at once, keeping a little for glazing.

6. Mix quickly into a soft dough.

7. Turn onto floured board; knead lightly and quickly.

8. Roll or press out to a round shape about 2 cm thick.

9. Cut into eight triangular pieces using a floured knife, or use a plain round 4.5 cm cutter.

10. Glaze with milk.

11. Cook quickly—8 to 10 minutes—in a hot oven, 230–260°C.

12. Cool.

METHOD 2

Follow Method 1 with the exception of steps 4 and 5. Instead, melt fat and make up to 1 cup liquid with milk.

METHOD 3

Roll scone mixture to cover greased pizza tray, spread with tomato paste, add a variety of sliced foods topped with grated mozzarella cheese. Bake for 15 minutes in a hot oven.

VARIATIONS

1. *Roll or press out the dough. Spread with grated cheese and sprinkle with salt and pepper. Roll up like a Swiss roll. Using a sharp knife cut into 1–2 cm pieces. Place on a well-greased slide, with the cut edge up. Bake as above.*

2. *Anchovy or ham paste may be used instead of cheese.*

Makes 18–24 small round scones

Note: Plain scone mixtures may be pressed out the size of saucepan or casserole and placed on top of stews or stewed fruits. Cook for 20 to 30 minutes with lid on tightly.

CHERRY AND NUT RING

INGREDIENTS

*2 cups self-raising flour
Pinch salt
90 g butter or margarine
⅓ cup sugar
1 egg
⅔ cup milk
½ cup chopped nuts
½ cup chopped cherries
½ teaspoon cinnamon*

METHOD

1. Sift flour and salt.
2. Rub in butter. Add sugar.
3. Beat egg and add to milk.
4. Add to other ingredients and mix into a soft dough.
5. Knead lightly and press or roll out to 1 cm thick.
6. Spread nuts, cherries and cinnamon on dough.
7. Roll lengthwise, form into a ring on a greased flat pan or in a greased ring pan.
8. Cut slices 2 cm wide almost through with a sharp knife or kitchen scissors.
9. Bake at 200–220°C for 20 to 25 minutes.

VARIATIONS

*Instead of nuts, cherries and cinnamon use:
(a) 1 cup mixed fruit and 2 teaspoons sugar; or
(b) 1 cup finely grated apple, ½ tablespoon sugar and 1 teaspoon grated lemon rind; or
(c) 1 cup finely chopped dates and 2 teaspoons brown sugar.*

PUFTALOONS (FRIED SCONES)

INGREDIENTS

1 cup self-raising flour
Pinch salt
½ cup milk
Clarified fat or oil

METHOD

1. Sift flour and salt.

2. Add milk nearly all at once, and make into a soft dough.

3. Turn onto a floured board and knead slightly.

4. Press out about 1 cm thick.

5. Cut with a small round floured cutter.

6. Make a small quantity of clarified fat moderately hot in a small frying pan.

7. Put the puftaloons in and fry gently until golden brown underneath, then turn with a knife and cook until the other side is browned.

8. Drain on absorbent paper.

9. Serve hot with honey, golden syrup or jam.

Makes 12

GEM SCONES

INGREDIENTS

2 tablespoons or 60 g butter or margarine
3 tablespoons sugar
1 egg
4 tablespoons milk
1¼ cups self-raising flour
¼ teaspoon salt

METHOD

1. Heat gem irons

2. Beat butter and sugar to a cream.

3. Add egg and beat well.

4. Add milk.

5. Add sifted flour and salt, and mix lightly.

6. Place into heated, greased gem irons.

7. Bake in a hot oven, 230–250°C, for 7 to 10 minutes.

Makes 18

PUMPKIN SCONES

INGREDIENTS

2 tablespoons or 60 g butter
2 tablespoons sugar
½ cup mashed pumpkin
1 egg
½ cup milk
2½ cups self-raising flour

METHOD

1. Cream butter and sugar.

2. Add pumpkin.

3. Add well-beaten egg.

4. Add milk slowly.

5. Add sifted flour.

6. Knead lightly on floured board.

7. Roll out 2–3 cm thick.

8. Cut into rounds.

9. Put on floured tray.

10. Bake at 230–260°C for 20 minutes.

11. Place on rack to cool.

Makes 16

COFFEE ROLLS

INGREDIENTS

90 g butter
½ cup sugar
1 egg (60 g)
1 cup milk
4 cups self-raising flour

METHOD

1. Cream butter and sugar.

2. Add beaten egg; beat well.

3. Add milk.

4. Stir in sifted flour.

5. Mix well to a soft dough.

6. Roll on a floured board to a thickness of 1 cm.

7. Cut into 8 cm rounds; glaze, fold and glaze.

8. Bake in hot oven, 230–260°C, for 10 minutes.

Makes 24

DATE OR SULTANA SCONES

INGREDIENTS

⅓ cup sultanas or dates
2 cups self-raising flour
¼ teaspoon salt
2 tablespoons or 60 g butter
3 tablespoons sugar
1 egg
⅔ cup milk

METHOD

1. Preheat oven.

2. Sprinkle a little flour on an oven slide or baking dish.

3. Wash, stem and dry sultanas or chop dates.

4. Sift flour and salt.

5. Rub in butter lightly with tips of fingers until quite free from lumps.

6. Add sugar and sultanas or dates.

7. Beat egg well, and add the milk to it.

8. Pour into the dry ingredients, nearly all at once, enough to make a moist dough. Leave a little for glazing.

9. Turn onto a floured board and knead lightly.

10. Roll or press out about 1–2 cm thick.

11. Stamp into rounds with a small cutter.

12. Glaze with the remainder of the egg and milk.

13. Place on prepared slide or baking dish.

14. Bake in a hot oven, 230–260°C, for about 12 minutes.

15. When cooked, turn onto a cooler.

VARIATIONS

1. *Add 1 tablespoon of finely grated orange rind instead of fruit.*

2. *Omit fruit from mixture and*
   (a) Roll or press out the dough.
   Glaze with milk.
   Sprinkle with brown sugar and mixed fruit.
   Roll up like a Swiss roll.
   Using a sharp knife cut into 1–2 cm pieces.
   Place on a well-greased slide, with cut edge up.

Bake as above.
*(b)   Cream 2 tablespoons
butter and 3 tablespoons
brown sugar.
Spread on dough, sprinkle
with cinnamon, and roll
out.
Cut and bake as above.*

Makes 16

DAMPER

INGREDIENTS

*500 g plain flour
½ level teaspoon bicarbonate
of soda
1 level teaspoon cream of
tartar
1 teaspoon salt
1¼ cups water*

METHOD

1. Sift dry ingredients into a bowl.

2. Add cold water to make a firm, yet soft dough.

3. Knead lightly on a floured board and shape into a circular loaf 5 cm thick.

4. Place on a greased baking tray and bake in a hot oven, 200–230°C, for 20 to 25 minutes.

5. Turn onto a cake cooler.

Note: (From *The Captain Cook Book* by Babette Hayes.) Originally dampers were cooked in the ashes of a fire. The ashes were raked flat and the damper was placed onto the ashes and cooked for 10 minutes. Then the damper was covered with ashes and cooked for a further 20 to 30 minutes. The damper was cooked when it sounded hollow when tapped with a blunt instrument. A lighter damper was made by cooking in a greased camp oven with ashes covering the lid.

VARIATIONS

*1. The basic dough may be divided into twenty pieces and shaped into rolls, plaits, twists or as desired.
2. Glaze with milk or egg glaze and sprinkle with sesame seeds, caraway seeds, poppy seeds, grated cheese or chopped bacon.*

DATE LOAF

INGREDIENTS

1 cup boiling water
1 cup chopped dates
1 tablespoon butter or
margarine
¾ cup sugar
1 egg
1 teaspoon bicarbonate of
soda
2 cups self-raising flour or a
mixture of self-raising
wholemeal and white flour

METHOD

1. Prepare a loaf pan.

2. Soak dates in boiling water.

3. Cream butter and sugar.

4. Beat egg and add slowly to butter and sugar, beating well.

5. Add soda to date mixture then stir into creamed mixture.

6. Stir in sifted flour until well mixed.

7. Place into two prepared pans, 25 cm × 9 cm × 5 cm, or two 17 cm round closed pans.

8. Bake 30 minutes in centre of moderate oven.

BREADS AND YEAST COOKERY

BROWN BREAD

INGREDIENTS

40 g (2 tablespoons)
compressed yeast
2 cups warm water
3 cups plain flour
1 tablespoon salt
3 cups fine wheatmeal
1 tablespoon sugar
1 tablespoon lard or butter

METHOD

1. Crumble yeast into a small basin.

2. Add ⅔ cup of the water, mix well, and set aside.

3. Sift flour and salt into a large basin.

4. Add wheatmeal and sugar. Mix well.

5. Rub in lard or butter.

6. Make a well in the centre of the flour mixture and pour in the yeast and water mixture.

7. Mix to a soft dough with the remaining water.

8. Turn out onto a floured board.

9. Knead well until the dough is smooth, satiny and not sticky. Dough is ready if it springs back when pressed lightly with a finger.

10. Form dough into a ball, cover with a clean cloth, and stand in a warm place for 10 minutes.

11. Knead dough lightly to break any large gas bubbles that may have formed.

12. Divide dough in half. Form each piece into a ball.

13. Place on a well-greased oven tray.

14. Cover with a cloth and a piece of plastic.

15. Stand in a warm place until dough has doubled in bulk—30 to 40 minutes.

16. Bake in a hot oven, 230–260°C, for 25 to 35 minutes.

Note: Dough may be moulded into loaves and baked in pans (see white bread (1) below). For wholemeal bread omit white flour and use 6 cups fine wheatmeal.

WHITE BREAD (1)

INGREDIENTS

20 g (1 tablespoon) compressed yeast or 1 tablespoon dried yeast
1 kg plain flour
1 tablespoon sugar
2½ cups warm water (variable)
1 tablespoon salt

METHOD

1. Combine yeast, 1 teaspoon sugar, 1 teaspoon flour and ½ cup warm water and stand in a warm place until bubbles appear.

2. Sift flour and combine with remainder of dry ingredients in warm basin and make a well in the centre.

3. Combine activated yeast mixture and remainder of warm water.

4. Pour into the well and mix with flour to a soft dough.

5. Turn onto a floured board or leave in the bowl.

6. Knead well until the dough is smooth, satiny and not sticky. Dough is ready if it springs back when pressed lightly with a finger.

7. Place in a warmed, greased basin. Turn dough over so the surface is greased.

8. Cover with a cloth and a piece of plastic to prevent surface drying.

9. Stand in a warm place until the dough has doubled in bulk—35 to 40 minutes.

10. Lift dough onto floured board.

11. Knead lightly to break any large gas bubbles.

12. Divide dough into three pieces (one for each pan).

13. Roll each out to a rectangle as wide as the pans are long.

14. Roll up like a Swiss roll starting from the short side. Seal the edge but not the ends.

15. Place in well-greased pans. Pans should be about half full.

16. Cover and let stand in a warm place until dough has risen above the tops of the pans—10 to 20 minutes.

17. Bake in a hot oven, 230–260°C, for 25 to 30 minutes. If cooked, the loaf will sound hollow when tapped on top.

18. Turn onto cake cooler, leave until cool.

WHITE BREAD (2) (WITH MILK)

INGREDIENTS

1¼ cups milk (or milk and water)
1 tablespoon sugar
500 g plain flour
1 tablespoon salt
1 tablespoon butter or lard
20 g (1 tablespoon) compressed yeast

METHOD

1. Scald milk, add sugar. Cool to lukewarm.

2. Sift flour and salt into a warm basin.

3. Rub in butter or lard.

4. Crumble yeast into milk and sugar mixture and stir well.

5. Make a well in the centre of the flour and pour in milk mixture.

6. Mix to a soft dough.

7. Turn onto a floured board.

8. Knead until dough is smooth and satiny—about 10 minutes.

9. Cover with a clean cloth and a piece of plastic, and stand in a warm place for 10 minutes.

10. Shape and mould as desired.

11. Place on greased trays. Cover with a cloth and a piece of plastic.

12. Stand in a warm place until dough has doubled in bulk.

13. Bake on the trays in a hot oven, 230–260°C, until well risen and golden—about 25 to 30 minutes. If cooked, bread will sound hollow when tapped on top.

Note: For dinner rolls, divide dough into 24 even-sized pieces.

STOLLEN

INGREDIENTS

1 tablespoon compressed yeast
3 tablespoons lukewarm water
3 cups plain flour
2 eggs
60 ml evaporated milk
½ cup sugar
1 teaspoon vanilla
⅛ teaspoon lemon essence
½ teaspoon salt
Pinch cardamom
125 g butter, melted
250 g (1½ cups) mixed dried fruit

METHOD

1. Dissolve yeast in water.

2. Add 3 tablespoons of the flour and mix well.

3. Cover and stand in a warm place for 25 minutes or until the sponge rises and falls back.

4. Beat eggs with evaporated milk, sugar, vanilla and lemon essence.

5. Sift remainder of the flour, salt and cardamom together into a basin.

6. Add milk mixture and sponge.

7. Mix well to make a soft dough.

8. Add melted butter. Mix until butter is incorporated and dough is smooth.

9. Turn onto a floured board.

10. Knead for 5 minutes.

11. Knead in mixed dried fruit, adding an extra tablespoon of flour if necessary.

12. Cover with a cloth and stand in a warm place for 10 minutes.

13. Divide dough into two pieces.

14. Roll each piece out to an oval shape on a lightly floured board.

15. Brush surface of each piece with a little melted butter.

16. Fold one rounded end over to within 2 cm of the opposite end.

17. Place on greased oven trays.

18. Cover each tray with a piece of plastic and a cloth.

19. Stand in a warm place until size almost doubles—approximately 30 minutes.

20. Bake in a moderate oven, 200–220°C, for 25 minutes or until well risen and golden brown.

21. Remove from oven, brush with melted butter and sprinkle with sugar flavoured with vanilla.

YEAST BUNS

INGREDIENTS

⅓ *cup skim milk powder*
⅓ *cup sugar*
1 *cup water*
90 *g butter*
40 *g (2 tablespoons) compressed yeast*
500 *g plain flour*
2 *teaspoons salt*
¼ *teaspoon cinnamon*
½ *teaspoon mixed spice*
½ *cup sultanas*

GLAZING

1 *teaspoon gelatine*
1 *tablespoon sugar*
1 *tablespoon hot water*

METHOD

1. Mix skim milk powder and sugar together in a saucepan. Add ⅔ cup of the water. Mix until smooth.

2. Heat, stirring constantly, until boiling.

3. Add butter and remaining water. Cool to lukewarm, then add crumbled yeast.

4. Sift flour, salt and spices together. Add sultanas.

5. Add milk mixture and mix well to make a soft dough (add more warm water if necessary).

6. Knead well for 10 minutes (dough should be satiny).

7. Place in a greased bowl, cover with plastic, and stand in a warm place for 10 minutes.

8. Divide dough into sixteen even-sized pieces. Shape into buns.

9. Place on greased slides, and stand in a warm place until they double in bulk—20 to 30 minutes.

10. Bake in a moderately hot oven, 200–230°C, for 15 to 20 minutes.

11. Glaze immediately with gelatine and sugar dissolved in the hot water.

Makes 16

SANDWICHES

TYPES

LUNCH PACK
Two slices of bread or pocket bread spread with butter or margarine and a generous layer of filling between.

TOASTED
Make as above, toast both sides and serve immediately. Crusts may be trimmed.

OPEN
One slice of bread with a firm crisp crust, spread with butter or margarine and covered with a variety of foods arranged attractively.

CLUB OR DOUBLE DECKER
Three or more slices of buttered bread or toast with a different filling for each layer.

FANCY SANDWICHES FOR AFTERNOON TEA OR PARTIES
Ribbon: Four slices of bread, two brown and two white. Butter bread, spread with smooth savoury filling. Arrange brown and white bread alternately. Press lightly, cut across into fingers and arrange on a plate to show the strips.
Pinwheels: Use unsliced sandwich loaf, remove crusts, slice thinly lengthwise, butter and spread with soft filling,

roll as for a Swiss roll. Wrap in plastic wrap or greaseproof paper. Chill, then slice.
Rolled Sandwiches: Remove crusts from slices of fresh sandwich loaves. Spread with creamed butter or margarine, cover with filling or place a length of asparagus. Roll up, secure with cocktail sticks, and chill. Remove sticks before serving.

GENERAL RULES FOR MAKING

1. Prepare bread.

2. Spread with softened butter, margarine, cream, cottage or ricotta cheese or mayonnaise.

3. Spread fillings generously.

4. Place second slice on top of filling, press lightly.

5. Trim edges if necessary.

6. Cut.

7. If for packed lunches then wrap in plastic film, greaseproof or waxed paper.

8. If for serving at home then arrange on plates, garnish with parsley sprigs, shredded lettuce or celery curls.

Note: Horseradish sauce, crushed garlic, prepared mustard, chopped herbs or relish may be added to softened spread.

FILLINGS

CHEESE Sliced or grated, plain or with chopped nuts, raisins, chives, parsley, celery, apple, grated carrot, pineapple, sliced cucumber, tomato or chutney.

CREAM CHEESE Beat until smooth then add chopped onion, celery, gherkins, capsicum, dates, raisins, ginger, nuts, pineapple, chopped ham, alfalfa, bean sprouts or a combination of any of these.

MEAT AND POULTRY Any cold, cooked meats, sliced thinly or minced and mixed with sauce or chutney.

FISH Flaked smoked fish
mixed with a little white
sauce and chopped parsley.
Tuna mixed with a little
mayonnaise or cream,
chopped gherkin or tomato.
Salmon, mixed with a little
lemon juice.
Sardines, mixed with a little
lemon juice.

EGGS Scrambled. For
variety add curry powder,
chives, parsley or chopped
bacon.

PEANUT BUTTER with
shredded cabbage, grated
carrot, mashed banana or
chopped raisins.

SANDWICH SPREADS

VEGETABLE EXTRACTS

SAUCES AND GRAVY

APPLE SAUCE

INGREDIENTS

2 apples
1 teaspoon lemon juice
1 tablespoon water
2 teaspoons butter
1 tablespoon sugar

METHOD

1. Peel, core and slice apples.

2. Put in a saucepan with lemon juice, water, butter and sugar.

3. Simmer until tender.

4. Beat with a wooden spoon until smooth.

5. Serve with roast pork, roast duck or goose.

HORSERADISH SAUCE

INGREDIENTS

1 root horseradish or 1 tablespoon powdered horseradish
3 tablespoons cream
2 tablespoons milk
1 teaspoon prepared mustard
2 teaspoons sugar
¼ teaspoon salt
Pinch white pepper
1 tablespoon vinegar

METHOD

1. Scrape horseradish finely and mix with cream, milk, mustard, sugar, salt and pepper.

2. Add vinegar a little at a time.

CARAMEL SAUCE

INGREDIENTS

1 cup brown sugar
2 tablespoons water
1 tablespoon butter
2 tablespoons condensed milk

METHOD

1. Place sugar, water and butter in a saucepan.

2. Stir over heat until sugar dissolves; boil for 1 minute.

3. Remove from heat and stir in condensed milk.

BREAD SAUCE

INGREDIENTS

1 cup milk
½ blade mace or bay leaf
1 shallot
4 tablespoons fresh white breadcrumbs
2 teaspoons butter
¼ teaspoon salt

METHOD

1. Put milk, mace and shallot into a saucepan and bring to the boil.

2. Strain.

3. Return milk to the saucepan.

4. Add breadcrumbs, butter and salt.

5. Beat well with a wooden spoon.

6. Return to stove and stir while reheating.

7. Serve with roast fowl.

CUSTARD SAUCE

INGREDIENTS

1 tablespoon custard powder
2 teaspoons sugar
1 cup milk

METHOD

1. Blend custard powder and sugar with a little milk.

2. Boil remainder of milk.

3. Add boiling milk to blended mixture, stirring well.

4. Return to saucepan and stir over heat until boiling.

5. Boil gently for 2 minutes.

CHERRY SAUCE

INGREDIENTS

2 tablespoons arrowroot
1 500 g can cherries
1 tablespoon lemon juice or vinegar

METHOD

1. Blend the arrowroot with 2 tablespoons of cherry syrup.

2. Place cherries with syrup and lemon juice into a saucepan and bring to the boil.

3. Stir in blended arrowroot and boil for 1 minute.

4. Serve hot or cold with roast duckling.

MINT SAUCE

INGREDIENTS

2 tablespoons chopped green mint
2 tablespoons white sugar
1 tablespoon boiling water
2 tablespoons vinegar

METHOD

1. Wash and dry mint, remove stalks.

2. Chop very finely.

3. Boil sugar and water for 1 minute.

4. Add mint and vinegar.

5. Pour into container to cool.

6. Stir well before serving.

7. Serve in a small glass jug as an accompaniment to roast lamb.

LEMON SAUCE

INGREDIENTS

1 tablespoon arrowroot or
1½ tablespoons cornflour
1 cup water
½ teaspoon grated lemon rind
1 tablespoon sugar
2 tablespoons lemon juice

METHOD

1. Blend arrowroot or cornflour with a little cold water.

2. Boil remaining water and lemon rind.

3. Add blended arrowroot/ cornflour, mix thoroughly, and stir until it boils and thickens. Cook for 3 minutes.

4. Remove from heat and add sugar and lemon juice.

5. Serve with stacked pancakes and steamed ginger or sponge puddings.

ORANGE SAUCE

INGREDIENTS

1 tablespoon cornflour
⅛ teaspoon freshly ground nutmeg
1 cup water
1 teaspoon grated orange rind
¼ cup orange juice
2 tablespoons lemon juice

METHOD

1. Blend the cornflour with 2 tablespoons of the water, add nutmeg and remainder of the water.

2. Place into a saucepan, bring to the boil, stirring all the time.

3. Remove from heat, add rind and juices.

4. Use with duck, pork or lamb.

SWEET WHITE SAUCE

INGREDIENTS

1 tablespoon maize cornflour
1 cup milk
1 tablespoon sugar
Vanilla essence

METHOD

1. Blend cornflour with a little milk.

2. Put remainder of milk and sugar on to boil in a saucepan.

3. When nearly boiling remove from the heat, add the blended cornflour, stirring it in with a wooden spoon.

4. Stir over heat for 3 minutes, add vanilla.

5. Serve as an accompaniment to puddings.

Basic White or Melted Butter Sauce

TYPE	BUTTER OR MARGARINE	FLOUR (PLAIN)	MILK	USE
1. Pouring or Thin	1 tablespoon	1 tablespoon	1 cup	Cream Soups
2. Medium	1½ tablespoons	1½ tablespoons	1 cup	Vegetables Boiled meats Fish Puddings
3. Thick or Masking	2 tablespoons	2 tablespoons	1 cup	Masking Sauce Souffles Scalloped foods Savoury fillings
4. Panada	3 tablespoons	3 tablespoons	1 cup	Binding Croquettes

Salt and pepper to taste.

METHOD

1. Melt butter or margarine in saucepan—do not brown.

2. Remove from heat, add flour—and salt and pepper to taste. Stir with wooden spoon until smooth.

3. Stir over low heat for 1 minute—it must not be allowed to brown.

4. Add milk.

5. Stir over heat until it boils and thickens.

VARIATIONS

PARSLEY SAUCE *Add two tablespoons finely chopped parsley.*
ONION SAUCE *Add ½ cup cooked chopped onion.*
CAPER SAUCE *Add 2 tablespoons capers.*
CHEESE SAUCE *Add ½ cup grated cheese.*
CURRY SAUCE *Add 2 teaspoons curry powder to flour.*
MUSTARD SAUCE *Add 2 teaspoons mustard to flour.*
ANCHOVY SAUCE *Add 2 teaspoons concentrated anchovy sauce or paste and ½ teaspoon lemon juice.*
SWEET SAUCE *Instead of salt and pepper add 1 tablespoon of sugar.*

BROWN GRAVY

INGREDIENTS

1 ½ tablespoons plain flour
Pinch pepper
¼ teaspoon salt
1 cup water or stock

METHOD

1. Strain most of the fat out of the baking dish or frying pan after cooking meat.

2. Add flour, pepper and salt to the dish or pan.

3. Brown over the heat, stirring with the back of a spoon.

4. When brown, add water or stock—all at once if cold; gradually if boiling or hot water is used.

5. Stir until boiling; if not sufficiently brown add a few drops of caramel (see p. 245) or beef extract.

6. Strain (if necessary) and serve.

TARTARE SAUCE

INGREDIENTS

1 cup mayonnaise
2 teaspoons chopped parsley
2 teaspoons chopped gherkin
2 teaspoons chopped capers
2 teaspoons chopped olives

METHOD

Mix all ingredients together adding more vinegar if necessary for desired consistency.

PEANUT SAUCE

INGREDIENTS

1 crushed clove garlic
½ cup crunchy peanut butter
2 tablespoons soy sauce
1 teaspoon brown sugar
Squeeze lemon juice
Pinch chilli powder
¼ cup water or coconut milk

METHOD

1. Combine ingredients in a medium-sized saucepan.

2. Stir over a moderate heat until smooth, then slowly stir in enough water or *coconut milk* to give a creamy dipping consistency.

3. Sauce may be made well ahead and stored in a covered jar in the refrigerator, ready to reheat.

PLAIN BROWN SAUCE

INGREDIENTS

1 tablespoon meat dripping or oil
1 onion
1 tablespoon plain flour
Pinch pepper
½ teaspoon salt
1 cup water or stock
1 tablespoon Worcestershire sauce
1 teaspoon vinegar

METHOD

1. Place dripping or oil in a small saucepan and heat.

2. Peel onion and cut into dice.

3. Fry onion until well browned but not burnt.

4. Drain the fat off.

5. Add flour, pepper and salt to the onion, and stir until it browns.

6. Add water or stock, all at once, and stir until it boils.

7. Add sauce and vinegar.

8. Simmer about 10 minutes.

9. Strain and serve hot as an accompaniment to cutlets, rissoles, sausage rolls, etc.

HOLLANDAISE SAUCE

INGREDIENTS

60 g butter
3 egg yolks
1 tablespoon white vinegar
Salt and pepper to taste

METHOD

1. The secret of this sauce is that it must not overboil.

2. Melt butter in a double saucepan or in a basin over hot water.

3. Combine egg yolks, vinegar, salt and pepper.

4. Add to melted butter. Stir briskly without stopping until the sauce is smooth and thick.

5. Test and add extra salt and pepper if necessary.

FRUIT PUREE

METHOD

1. Allow 500 g fruit for each 250 ml of puree.

2. Fruit may be raw, cooked, canned or frozen.

3. If cooking the fruit use a small amount of water.

4. Canned fruit should be drained.

5. The puree is made by rubbing the fruit through a sieve or using an electric blender.

6. The puree can be used to make a fool, a coulis or sauce or made into a snow.

CHUTNEY, PICKLES AND BOTTLED SAUCES

APPLE CHUTNEY

INGREDIENTS

5 large cooking apples
500 g onions
1½ cups sultanas or raisins
500 g brown sugar
3 cups vinegar
½ cup water
2 teaspoons dry mustard
2 teaspoons salt
¼ teaspoon cayenne pepper
¼ teaspoon black pepper

METHOD

1. Peel apples and onions. Cut into small pieces.

2. Place in saucepan with all other ingredients.

3. Stir over heat until boiling.

4. Cook slowly—at least 2 hours.

5. Bottle in warm jars and seal when cool.

CHOKO CHUTNEY

INGREDIENTS

1 kg chokoes
½ tablespoon salt
2 cups vinegar
30 g chillies
4 cloves garlic
30 g whole ginger
500 g brown sugar
⅔ cup sultanas

METHOD

1. Peel chokoes and cut into long strips. Sprinkle

with salt and let stand overnight.

2. Boil vinegar, add chokoes and simmer until soft.

3. Cut chillies, garlic and ginger into small pieces.

4. Add with sugar and sultanas to the chokoes and vinegar.

5. Simmer gently until clear and rich brown in colour—about 2 hours.

6. Bottle in warm jars and seal when cool.

MUSTARD PICKLE

INGREDIENTS

1 kg cauliflower or chokoes or green tomatoes, or a mixture of all three
500 g onions
250 g beans
1 tablespoon salt
Enough vinegar to cover vegetables (3–4 cups)
½ teaspoon mixed spice
1 cup golden syrup
12 cloves
12 peppercorns

1 tablespoon mustard
1 tablespoon curry powder
1 tablespoon plain flour

METHOD

1. Wash and prepare vegetables. Cut into convenient-size pieces.

2. Place in basin, sprinkle with salt, and let stand overnight.

3. Put vinegar, spice and syrup on to boil, adding cloves and peppercorns tied in a muslin bag.

4. Drain vegetables. Add to boiling vinegar.

5. Boil for 20 minutes or until crisp. Remove bag.

6. Blend mustard, curry powder and flour with extra vinegar.

7. Add to saucepan, stir and simmer for 10 minutes.

8. Bottle in warm jars and seal when cool.

PLUM SAUCE

INGREDIENTS

3 kg plums
1.5 kg white sugar
½ teaspoon pepper
¼ teaspoon cayenne pepper
5 cups vinegar
1 tablespoon salt
1 onion
1 tablespoon ground ginger

METHOD

1. Wash plums.

2. Place all ingredients in pan; stir until sugar dissolves.

3. Boil until stones separate from fruit.

4. Strain through a coarse strainer and bottle in warm jars.

5. Cork or seal when sauce is cold.

TOMATO SAUCE

INGREDIENTS

3 kg ripe tomatoes
250 g apples
250 g onions
2 cloves garlic
1 cup sugar
2 tablespoons salt
1 chilli
½ tablespoon cloves
½ tablespoon peppercorns
1 teaspoon curry powder
2½ cups vinegar

METHOD

1. Wash tomatoes and cut up roughly.

2. Peel and slice apples and onions.

3. Cut garlic up finely.

4. Place in saucepan; add all other ingredients.

5. Boil gently for 2 hours.

6. Press through a coarse strainer. Return to heat and boil to reduce liquid by a third of quantity.

7. Bottle and seal.

TOMATO RELISH

INGREDIENTS

1.5 kg tomatoes
500 g onions
2 cups sugar
2½ cups vinegar
1 tablespoon flour
1 tablespoon curry powder
Pinch cayenne
1 tablespoon dry mustard
1 tablespoon salt

METHOD

1. Cut up tomatoes and pour off ¾ cup of juice.

2. Cut up onions finely.

3. Put in a saucepan with tomatoes, sugar and vinegar.

4. Boil slowly until it thickens.

5. Blend flour, curry powder, cayenne, mustard and salt with tomato juice.

6. Add to saucepan and stir until boiling.

7. Cook gently for 3 minutes.

8. Bottle in warm jars and seal when cool.

JAMS AND JELLIES

To ensure success the fruit should be firm, sound and slightly under-ripe. Early fruits are best for jam-making. As a general rule, 1½ cups sugar are used to each 500 g of fruit, or 1 cup sugar to each cup of pulp when making jam, and 1 cup sugar to 1 cup juice for jelly.

Pectin test: Before adding sugar take 1 tablespoon juice from cooked fruit, cool and add 3 tablespoons methylated spirits. If a single firm clot forms there is sufficient pectin for the jam to jell. If the clot is broken the mixture needs to have lemon juice or commercial pectin added to it.

To test if cooked: Place a small quantity on a cold saucer; cool. If cooked it will jell and wrinkle when moved.

CARROT AND LEMON JAM

INGREDIENTS

500 g carrots
3 lemons
2 litres water
2 kg sugar

METHOD

1. Grate carrots and slice lemons thinly.

2. Cover with water and let stand overnight.

3. Bring to the boil and boil, covered, for 1¼ hours.

4. Add sugar, stir until dissolved.

5. Boil until the jam jells when tested, about ¾ to 1 hour.

6. Bottle in warm jars and seal.

7. Boil until the jam will jell when tested.

8. Pour into heated jars and seal.

VARIATIONS

Pineapple or passionfruit may be added instead of ginger.

TOMATO JAM

INGREDIENTS

2 kg tomatoes
3 lemons
3 tablespoons preserved ginger
1.75 kg sugar

METHOD

1. Wash tomatoes. Cut into pieces.

2. Peel lemons finely and cut the peel into thin shreds.

3. Grate or chop the ginger.

4. Squeeze juice from lemons.

5. Place tomatoes, ginger, sugar, lemon peel and lemon juice in saucepan.

6. Stir over heat until boiling.

BLACKBERRY JAM

INGREDIENTS

500 g blackberries
1½ cups sugar

METHOD

1. Remove stalks from berries and place in saucepan.

2. Cover with sugar and allow to stand about 1 hour.

3. Place over heat, stir occasionally until sugar is dissolved.

4. Boil until the jam jells when tested.

5. Bottle in warm jars and seal.

APPLE JELLY

INGREDIENTS

Slightly under-ripe apples
Sugar (1 cup for each cup of juice)

METHOD

1. Wash the apples, slice, and just cover with water.

2. Boil gently until soft—30 to 40 minutes.

3. Strain through a jelly flannel or clean linen cloth fastened securely above a basin.

4. Allow to drip through slowly. *Do not* squeeze.

5. Measure out one cup of sugar to each cup of juice.

6. Warm sugar in the oven and add to boiling liquid.

7. Stir over heat until sugar dissolves.

8. Boil quickly; test frequently until it jells when tested.

9. Remove any scum as it rises.

10. Pour into warm jars, seal and label.

Note: Crab-apples may be used with this recipe. Remove stalks and wash apples but do not cut.

DRIED APRICOT JAM

INGREDIENTS

500 g dried apricots
2 litres water
1.5 kg sugar

METHOD

1. Wash apricots.

2. Cover with water and allow to soak overnight or until soft.

3. Bring to the boil; cook gently until tender.

4. Add sugar heated in the oven.

5. Stir carefully until the sugar is dissolved.

6. Cook quickly until the mixture jells when tested.

7. Pour into heated jars.

8. Seal and label.

MARMALADE

INGREDIENTS

1 kg fruit
1 kg sugar
2 litres water

METHOD

1. Wash and slice fruit thinly; remove the seeds, centre pith and thick ends.

2. Place in a container, cover with water, and let stand overnight.

3. Boil fruit and water, covered, until rind is soft—about 1 hour.

4. Add sugar all at once; stir until dissolved.

5. Boil until it will jell when tested.

6. Bottle in warm jars and seal.

Note: Seeds and end pieces from fruit may be brought to boil in a small qauntity of water, strained and the water added before boiling fruit and water. Any citrus fruits or a mixture of citrus fruits may be used. The marmalade will be named accordingly.

PLUM JAM

INGREDIENTS

2 kg plums
1.5 kg sugar

METHOD

1. Wash plums; remove stones if possible.

2. Cook with a little of the sugar until fruit is tender.

3. Add the remaining sugar, heated in the oven.

4. When sugar is dissolved, cook rapidly until the jam will jell when tested.

5. Pour into heated jars and seal.

Note: Peaches, apricots or nectarines may be used instead of plums.

STRAWBERRY JAM

INGREDIENTS

Equal quantities of strawberries and sugar
¼ level teaspoon citric acid to every 2 kg fruit

METHOD

1. Remove stalks, wash strawberries.

2. Cook strawberries until soft (about 5 minutes), stirring gently.

3. Add warmed sugar and citric acid and boil for about 10 minutes until jells when tested.

4. Bottle in warm jars, seal, label and date.

SWEETS AND CONFECTIONERY

CREAMY COCONUT ICE

INGREDIENTS

125 g copha
500 g icing sugar
250 g coconut
1 teaspoon vanilla
2 egg whites
Pink colouring

METHOD

1. Melt copha in a saucepan.

2. Sift icing sugar into a basin and add coconut, vanilla and egg whites.

3. Stir in melted copha (not boiling) and mix well.

4. Line a square cake pan with greaseproof paper and spread one half of the mixture.

5. Colour the remainder of the mixture with pink colouring and spread over the white layer in the cake pan.

6. Stand in a cool place to set.

7. Cut into squares.

APPLES ON STICKS

INGREDIENTS

6 red apples
6 wooden skewers
1 cup cold water
500 g sugar
2 tablespoons vinegar

METHOD

1. Grease an oven slide.

2. Wash and dry apples. Place a skewer through the core of each.

3. Boil water, sugar and vinegar to 154°C measured on sweets thermometer, or until syrup turns golden brown.

4. Stand saucepan in a basin of hot water.

5. Dip apples in toffee and coat well.

6. Place on greased slide to set.

MARSHMALLOWS

INGREDIENTS

3 tablespoons gelatine
1 cup cold water
4 cups sugar
1½ cups hot water
Vanilla or lemon essence to taste
Icing sugar
Cornflour

METHOD

1. Soak gelatine in cold water.

2. Bring sugar and hot water to boiling point.

3. Add soaked gelatine.

4. Boil gently for 20 minutes.

5. Pour into a large mixing bowl. Cool and add essence.

6. Beat until thick.

7. Pour into wetted 28 cm × 18 cm slab cake pan.

8. When cold, cut into squares and toss in a mixture of icing sugar and cornflour, or plain or toasted coconut.

GINGER OR CHERRY CREAMS

INGREDIENTS

½ cup milk
2 cups sugar
Pinch cream of tartar
¾ cup preserved ginger or
cherries
2 teaspoons butter

METHOD

1. Place milk and sugar in saucepan.

2. Stir over low heat until sugar dissolves and the mixture boils.

3. Add cream of tartar and cherries or ginger.

4. Stir and bring to boiling point. Add butter.

5. Remove spoon. Boil for 6 minutes.

6. Cool slightly, then stir until mixture thickens.

7. Press into pans lined with waxed or greaseproof paper.

8. When cold, cut into pieces.

FRENCH JELLIES

INGREDIENTS

4 tablespoons powdered
gelatine
2 cups cold water
4 cups sugar
Pinch cream of tartar
2 teaspoons essence
Icing sugar

METHOD

1. Soak gelatine in half the water.

2. Place rest of water, sugar and cream of tartar in saucepan.

3. Bring to boil, stirring gently until sugar is dissolved.

4. Add gelatine and simmer gently for 20 minutes. Stir in essence.

5. Pour into wetted plates or pans.

6. When cold, cut into squares and toss in icing sugar.

COCONUT ICE

INGREDIENTS

½ cup milk
2 cups sugar
Pinch cream of tartar
½ cup desiccated coconut

METHOD

1. Put milk, sugar and cream of tartar into saucepan.

2. Stir over low heat until sugar dissolves and the mixture boils.

3. Remove spoon. Boil for 5 minutes.

4. Cool slightly, then beat well.

5. When beginning to thicken, add coconut and continue beating until mixture is quite thick.

6. Pour into a greased cake pan.

7. When cold, cut into squares.

UNCOOKED FONDANT

INGREDIENTS

2 teaspoons glucose
1 egg white
500 g pure icing sugar
¼ teaspoon lemon juice
3 drops vanilla
Food colouring

METHOD

1. Melt glucose in cup standing in boiling water.

2. Drop slightly beaten egg white into centre of icing sugar. Cover with a little icing sugar.

3. Add glucose and stir well with a wooden spoon.

4. When sugar is almost absorbed, turn onto a board dusted with icing sugar and knead until smooth.

5. Add flavourings and colouring.

PLAIN TOFFEE

INGREDIENTS

2 cups sugar
¾ cup cold water
1 tablespoon vinegar

METHOD

1. Place all ingredients in saucepan.

2. Stir over heat until sugar is dissolved.

3. Bring to boil—do not stir.

4. Cook until syrup is golden brown.

5. Remove from heat, allow bubbles to settle.

6. Pour into small paper containers or into a flat greased pan and mark into squares.

MISCELLANEOUS

BARLEY WATER

INGREDIENTS

2 tablespoons pearl barley
2½ cups boiling water
A small piece lemon rind

METHOD

1. Wash barley.

2. Put into the saucepan of boiling water.

3. Add lemon rind.

4. Boil without lid until reduced to half quantity.

5. Strain.

6. Sweeten to taste and add a little lemon juice.

SEASONING (STUFFING)

INGREDIENTS

1 small onion
1 cup white breadcrumbs
Pinch herbs
1 tablespoon butter
¼ teaspoon salt
Pinch pepper
1 tablespoon chopped parsley

METHOD

1. Blanch the onion by putting it in cold water and bringing to the boil.

2. Drain the water off, put into fresh boiling water, and cook until tender.

3. Drain in a colander.

4. Chop the onion finely and put into a basin.

5. Add all the other ingredients and mix well.

Note: This is used for seasoning duck, goose, pork and turkey.

LEMON DRINK

INGREDIENTS

1 lemon per person
1 teaspoon sugar per person
¼ cup boiling water
½ cup cold water

METHOD

1. Wash lemon.

2. Peel off zest only.

3. Place in jug with sugar.

4. Add boiling water to dissolve sugar.

5. When cold strain.

6. Squeeze juice from lemon and combine with cold water and lemon syrup.

Note: Use oranges or equal quantities of lemons and oranges. Keep covered in refrigerator. Can be made into ice blocks.

FORCEMEAT

INGREDIENTS

4 tablespoons white breadcrumbs
2 tablespoons butter or minced suet
1 tablespoon chopped parsley
¼ teaspoon mixed chopped thyme and marjoram
A little grated lemon rind and nutmeg
¼ teaspoon salt
Pinch pepper
1 well-beaten egg

METHOD

1. Mix all ingredients, except egg, well together.

2. Add beaten egg and stir well.

Note: This may be used for fowls, turkeys, rabbit and veal. For a turkey, mix ½ cup sausage meat with the forcemeat.

VARIATIONS

Pine nuts, pistachios, pecans, cashews and walnuts may be added to the basic recipe.

SWEET OMELETTE

INGREDIENTS

3 eggs
1 teaspoon water
1 tablespoon sugar
Jam
Butter

METHOD

1. Take yolks of 2 eggs and whites of 3 eggs.

2. Boil water and sugar, cool, and add to the yolks.

3. Beat whites stiffly.

4. Have ready a hot plate and some heated jam.

5. Heat omelette pan slowly.

6. Add the yolks to the whites and mix lightly.

7. Melt butter in pan and pour in the mixture.

8. Cook gently and shake occasionally until set.

9. When coloured slightly underneath, brown the top by placing in the oven or under the griller.

10. Lift onto a hot plate.

11. Spread heated jam on one half.

12. Fold the other half over.

13. Serve at once.

Serves 2

SAGE AND ONION STUFFING

INGREDIENTS

2 large onions
½ cup dry breadcrumbs
salt and pepper to taste
1 teaspoon dried sage

METHOD

1. Peel and chop onions finely and place in a saucepan.

2. Cover with boiling water and cook for 5 minutes or until tender.

3. Drain and mix with other ingredients.

4. Use for stuffing as desired.

BREAD AND MILK

INGREDIENTS

1 ¼ cups milk
1 thick slice of bread
1 teaspoon sugar (optional)

METHOD

1. Remove crusts and cut bread into 1 cm cubes.

2. Heat milk in a saucepan, add sugar, and pour over bread.

3. Serve hot.

Serves 1

CARAMEL

INGREDIENTS

2 level tablespoons sugar
⅔ cup water

METHOD

1. Place the sugar with 1 teaspoon of the water in a small saucepan (an old steel or iron one is best).

2. Cook until it becomes dark brown all over.

3. Add remainder of the water; allow to simmer very gently until the consistency of treacle—about 15 minutes.

4. Allow to cool, and pour into a wide-necked glass jar or bottle.

MAITRE D'HOTEL BUTTER OR GREEN BUTTER

INGREDIENTS

125 g butter
1 tablespoon chopped parsley
¼ teaspoon salt
A little cayenne (optional)
2 teaspoons lemon juice

METHOD

1. Soften butter. Mix with chopped parsley, salt and pepper.

2. Add lemon juice gradually mixing until smooth.

Note: This is used for steak, grilled cutlets or grilled fish.

HOMEMADE YOGHURT

INGREDIENTS

1 litre milk
1 cup natural yoghurt
empty jars

METHOD

1. Pour the milk into a saucepan and heat until bubbles appear around the edge. Do not allow to boil.

2. Heat milk for 15 minutes.

3. Cool milk until it is lukewarm—just a little warmer than a finger.

4. Stir in the yoghurt and pour the mixture into sterilised empty jars.

5. Close the lids tightly.

6. Place the jars in a large boiler or saucepan and fill it with hot water from the tap.

7. Wrap the pot in a bath towel to keep it warm.

8. Wait at least 5 hours then open the jars to see if the mixture has thickened, then chill the yoghurt.

9. Reserve 1 cup of the yoghurt to make the next quantity.

GHEE

INGREDIENTS

250 g unsalted butter

METHOD

1. Place butter in a saucepan and heat until the butter has melted and is frothy.

2. Discard the froth by spooning and pour melted butter into a basin. Cool.

3. Remove fat from the top leaving residue in basin.

4. Reheat fat and strain through muslin to remove remaining solids.

CLARIFIED FAT

INGREDIENTS

250 g mixed fat or suet
1 cup water

METHOD

1. Remove any small pieces of meat from the fat.

2. Cut fat into small pieces, about 2 cm square.

3. Place in a large saucepan.

4. Add the water, and cook slowly for ½ hour with lid on.

5. Remove the lid and stir frequently until all the water has evaporated.

6. Continue cooking and stirring until the fat is melted and appears like a clear oil.

7. Strain, pressing the pieces well to extract all fat.

8. Allow to cool—it should then be very hard and white.

COLOURED SUGAR

METHOD

Place 1 drop of colouring on 1 tablespoon of crystallised sugar, and mix well with the back of a spoon until a uniform colour. Coloured sugar is sprinkled over puddings which have egg white piled on top.

BREADCRUMBS

METHOD

1. For white breadcrumbs, rub the crumb part of stale bread through a sieve or colander, or use a blender.

2. For brown breadcrumbs, place crusts of bread and stale pieces in a very slow oven, and allow them to dry thoroughly. Place in plastic bag and crush on a board with a rolling pin until very fine. Store in glass jars or bottles.

TO BLEND FLOUR

INGREDIENTS

2 level tablespoons flour
⅔ cup milk or water

METHOD

1. Put the flour into a small basin.

2. Make a well in the centre and gradually stir in the liquid, using a wooden spoon.

3. Mix until quite smooth.

TO BEAT EGG WHITE

METHOD

1. Put the egg white on a flat dinner plate and use a dinner knife.

2. Hold the plate quite level, and while beating, keep the knife flat on the plate.

3. Beat quickly, keeping as much of the egg as possible moving over the knife at one time, until quite stiff.

RED WINE MARINADE

INGREDIENTS

¾ cup red wine
1 clove garlic, crushed
1 thinly sliced onion
2 tablespoons oil
1 crumbled bayleaf
2 tablespoons white vinegar
3 tablespoons Worcestershire sauce
Salt and pepper to taste

METHOD

1. Mix all ingredients together.

2. Use for beef or lamb.

3. Marinate meat for 12 to 48 hours in the refrigerator, turning occasionally.

TO CHOP HERBS

METHOD

1. Wash the herbs and dry well.

2. Pick the leaves off the stalks.

3. Gather the herbs tightly

in the fingers and cut with a sharp knife.

4. Do this several times, then hold the point of the knife downwards on the board and chop with the end nearest the handle until very fine.

FRUIT MARINADE

INGREDIENTS

¾ *cup orange juice*
2 *tablespoons honey*
2 *tablespoons vinegar*
1 *finely chopped onion*
3 *tablespoons grated orange rind*
½ *teaspoon thyme leaves*
Pinch ground cloves
¼ *teaspoon ground ginger*
Salt and pepper to taste

METHOD

1. Combine all ingredients.

2. Use for chicken or pork.

3. Marinate meat for 12 to 48 hours in the refrigerator, turning occasionally.

SPECIAL DIETS

Generally, recipes included in this book are appropriate for all members of the family including children, the aged and the convalescent.

CHILDREN—As soon as children are able to chew and digest solid food, their meals should consist of modified portions of those eaten by the rest of the family. Emphasis should be given to eating a variety of foods so that the child's nutrient needs are met.

THE AGED should choose a nutritious diet from a variety of foods. Because the aged are generally less active, emphasis should be given to selecting a diet which provides fewer kilojoules.

THE CONVALESCENT—Food selected should be easily digested because the digestive system is usually impaired by illness. The appetite needs to be stimulated by light and attractive meals served in small portions.

Children, the aged and convalescents could be served such dishes as:

INDEX

A worthy companion to the classic *Commonsense Cookery Book* — Book 1, this second volume maintains the clear, simple instructions that have made Book 1 so useful to beginners and experienced cooks alike.

The recipes are slightly more advanced: the great classic dishes of the world are included — Beef Stronganoff, Chicken Marengo, Crepes Suzette, Quiche Lorraine — all explained so thoroughly and simply that even a novice cook can be sure of success.

Also included is helpful information on cuts of meat, basic kitchen requisites, cookery terms and the use of microwave ovens.